CONVERSATIONS WITH WOMEN WHO EXPORT:
Inspiration, Motivation, and Strategy

STORIES OF WOMEN WHO . . .

"Took Roads Less Traveled By...and Made All the Difference"

by

SHARON T. FREEMAN, Ph.D.
President
All American Small Business Exporters Association, Inc.

Published by:
All American Small Business Exporters Association, Inc.
AASBEA
http://www.aasbea.com

We would like to acknowledge the following publishers for permission to reprint:

Risky Business. From the Los Angeles Times. © 1998 by Don Lee. Reprinted by permission of the Wall Street Journal, Eastern E. Dow Jones & Co., Inc.

In Tbilisi, It's Betsys Place: An Isle of Elegance Amid Byzantine Chaos. © 1997. Reprinted by permission of the International Herald Tribune.

Conversations With Women Who Export: Inspiration, Motivation, and Strategy
by Sharon T. Freeman, Ph.D.

ISBN 0-9703463-0-1 (trade paper)

1. Women—Business—Anecdotes.   1. Freeman, Sharon (date)

Library of Congress Card Number: 00-191976

Publisher:
All American Small Business Exporters Association, Inc.
2300 M Street, NW, Suite 800
Washington, DC 20037

Cover design by Visual Access.

The Road Not Taken

Two roads diverged in a yellow wood,
And sorry I could not travel both
And be one traveler, long I stood
And looked down one as far as I could
To where it bent in the undergrowth;

Then took the other, as just as fair,
And having perhaps the better claim,
Because it was grassy and wanted wear;
Though as for that, the passing there
Had worn them really about the same,

And both that morning equally lay
In leaves no step had trodden black.
Oh, I kept the first for another day!
Yet knowing how way leads on to way,
I doubted if I should ever come back.

I shall be telling this with a sigh
Somewhere ages and ages hence:
Two roads diverged in a wood, and I—
I took the one less traveled by,
And that has made all the difference.

– Robert Frost

I dedicate this book to the business women of the world.
May these stories help to inspire you, motivate you, and provide
strategic advice to you as you go global!

I also dedicate this book to all the wonderful people who have
helped to make this book possible.
May these stories similarly touch your hearts and inspire your souls.

Finally, I dedicate this book to my 80 year old mother, Sylvia
Freeman, my role model, whose entrepreneurship and business
savvy served as a beacon and shinning light guiding my path
throughout my life.

TABLE OF CONTENTS

ACKNOWLEDGMENTS

Conversations With Women Who Export: Inspiration, Motivation, and Strategy has taken more than a year to write, compile, and edit. It has been a true labor of love for all of the women featured in this book and for our supporters. One of the greatest joys in creating this book has been getting to know the women who have shared their stories. They gave their hearts and souls to this endeavor, and they did so on blind faith, as this initiative is without precedence. Each woman was willing to tell her story, even about the parts that were not so pleasant, in order to create a community of sharing with other women business owners. None of the women in this book have had an easy road; indeed, many of us are still striving, exploring, and trying to be the best at what we do. Despite everyone's busy schedules, all took the time to pause, reflect, and to share their stories. As is the case for all trailblazers in any endeavor, the women in this book have often been alone, traveling *roads less traveled*. It has been therapeutic for each of us to have someone with whom to share our stories and to create a community of sharing and giving that has made each of us feel a little less lonely.

I also would like to acknowledge and thank Edie Fraser, President of the Business Women's Network (BWI), who provided a forum through which I first met a number of the women in this book.

I also would like to acknowledge and thank my husband for his support for this book.

Finally, I would like to thank the readers for their interest in this work and for lending us their ears, empathy, and support!

SHARE WITH US

We would love to hear your reactions to the stories in this book. Please let us know whether we succeeded in inspiring, motivating, and informing you—also, let us know whether you found a little bit of yourself and your experiences in some of these stories and whether you have or will be *going global!*

We also invite you to consider participating in future editions of *Conversations With Women Who Export: Inspiration, Motivation, and Strategy*. Please send me an email at: aasbea@aol.com or feel free to send me information about yourself and your firm's accomplishments in the global arena to:

Dr. Sharon T. Freeman
President
All American Small Business Exporters Association, Inc. (AASBEA)
2300 M Street, NW, Suite 800
Washington, DC 20037
USA

Email: aasbea.@aol.com
Telephone: (202) 332-5137
Fax: (202) 332-5286

To order on online, please visit our website at:
http://www.aasbea.com

We also invite you to join our **All American Small Business Exporter Association**, Inc. to receive in-depth export counseling and up-to-date "need-to-know" information about exporting.

We hope you enjoy reading this book as much as we enjoyed compiling it, editing it, writing it, and telling our stories.

Conversations With Women Who Export: Inspiration, Motivation, and Strategy

Introduction

There is a road that each of us has followed in our dreams and that at each junction in life we wish to follow once again. Unhindered by the limitations of distance and expense, you'll find here the opportunity to roam the roads that the women in this book have traveled in their dreams and in their business lives.

The stories in this book explore the souls and lives of the women who followed their dreams and traveled roads less traveled. Discover a wealth of inspirational and informative insights into the strategies that the women featured in this book have pursued in *going global*.

About the Book

This book came into being because so many women have approached me over the years at my various workshops and speaking engagements on exporting to ask, *"How did you go global?"* This text provides an answer to that question by women of various ethnic backgrounds, in different industry segments, who are at different stages of export development. It offers insights into what it has taken, both personally and professionally, for each of us to go global.

The woman in this book were chosen for inclusion on the basis of the referral of associations, government agencies, and of people in the know. Our criteria included that the woman be the owner of her own business, that she be the one who made the decision to go global, and that her story be interesting, both from a professional and personal standpoint. All of the women in this book meet these criteria, and each has a unique and intensely personal story to tell about her experience. Indeed, there is no model for telling such stories: so many considerations both internal to the firm and external to the firm may have a bearing on the experience. Rather than to ask a pre-determined list of questions, we went with the flow of these stories as they unfolded. While each woman has determined what is important to share about her experience, one important recurring theme that emerged was the feeling of loneliness that each woman felt as she broke away from the pack and charted her global path. There is special meaning in Robert Frost's words "Two roads diverged in a wood, and I—I took the one less traveled by" for each of the women in this book, as you will see when you read their stories.

The women in this book have taken a detour off of their lonely roads to share their stories. Although most of the women in this book did not know each other prior to their participation in this book, you will find common threads among their stories: their high tolerance for risk and uncertainty and strong and well-founded sense of self-confidence, their concerns about doing things harmoniously, and their constant reinvestments into their businesses and in themselves to upgrade their skills and knowledge. You will also find that all of the women love a challenge and embrace change and the new technologies that help them to master change.

Although the women in this book are from many different ethnic backgrounds, including African and White American, Mexican-American, Colombian-American, Indian, and Swiss, you will find that their stories are similar. You will also find that if they were minorities that being so did not pose any special constraints to their ability to succeed and thrive in the global market place. To the contrary, in many cases, their ethnic backgrounds have helped them to embrace foreign cultures and to be embraced by them.

The family backgrounds of the women in this book did not necessarily have a bearing on their propensity to be entrepreneurial or on the likelihood that they would pursue global businesses. In some cases, women came from families where there is a tradition of entrepreneurship. Other woman in this book blazed a new trail. To the extent that the woman have taken advantage of the wealth of resources available from the U.S. government to assist them in going global, they have been able to travel faster on the road of global business expansion. Reading between the lines, you will also glean that going global has provided unparallel opportunities for the women to expand both their business and personal horizons and to gain further credibility as entrepreneurs. One of the strongest and most important motivations for each woman was to be the best at what she does. The drive toward excellence forms an integral part of how each of the women sees the world: not only to do business the best but to help make the world a better place in which to live.

The stories in this book also afford opportunities to learn from the mistakes that some of the women have made. The most common one, the failure to properly plan the export venture, stemmed from the feeling of invincibility that some of the women have developed because of their triumphs in the domestic market. They are so used to winning and moving quickly that when they turn their attention to new ventures in the global marketplace, they fail to take the time required to properly plan the venture. Global business cannot be successfully undertaken without devoting the time that is required to fully research and plan the endeavor. As you will see in these stories, simply hiring someone to handle the global business is not a shortcut. The business owner must understand the operations and mechanics of exporting in order to ensure that he or she can master the global domain in the same way that he or she has mastered her domestic market domain.

One final and important observation is that although the women in this book have been used to doing things alone, when they opt for going global they have to widen their circles and embrace the advice, experience, and cultures of others. Indeed their stories show us that it is not possible to go global alone. When the women in this book broaden their spheres to take advice from U.S. government agencies, from Chambers of Commerce, and from women's groups, they became more successful and their global businesses expanded. Perhaps in this regard, going global serves an invaluable purpose in connecting women to others with whom they can share their roads less traveled!

About the Women and their Stories in this Book

Sharon Freeman is an exporter of consulting services who wins the prize for the most improbable entry into the world of international business by establishing her first business in Hong Kong in the mid-1980s, and for having undertaken consulting assignments in more countries, across more borders than perhaps any other consultant, male or female. Having performed consulting assignments in over 100 countries, she is an example to other African American and minority woman demonstrating that all things are possible with the proper preparation, dedication, and belief in oneself.

Maria de Lourdes Sobrino, an exporter and manufacturer of gelatin, breaks the "mold" in many ways. She shows us that a first-generation Mexican can come to this country as an immigrant from an upper middle-class family in Mexico without having any friends and family in business and start a manufacturing business from scratch in America. She also shows us what happens when a dormant and innate entrepreneurial spirit is unharnessed. Once Maria connected with her entrepreneurial spirit, she was able to grow her business into a $10 million enterprise. Tragedies such as the breakup of her marriage and the breakup with her business partner never daunted her spirits, she continues to thrive and face each day with anticipation and excitement as she continues to create new global pathways in business.

Candace Chen is an exporter of an innovative, patented invention that improves the efficiency of engines. She shows us how going global can help to improve one's domestic market. She demonstrates how a young Chinese American woman who went to law school and never intended to become an exporter can nevertheless succeed in the global marketplace with the right planning, business tactics, and strategies. Candace has succeeded in business, not in spite of her strong sense of moral and professional ethics, but because of them. She also lifts our spirits by showing us that siblings can work together and support each other.

Martha Montoya is an exporter of a syndicated cartoon strip. Her notoriety comes from dreaming such an impossible dream in the first place: that of being a cartoonist when she could not even draw when she started out! She also has taken the most circuitous route to her present business, coming all the way from Colombia and working in many different capacities before succeeding in the American market and subsequently in global markets. She also shows us that dreams really do come true—and when they do, they really pay off.

Gisele Rufer is a manufacturer and exporter of Swiss-made women's watches. She no doubt traveled the furthest distance to break the glass ceiling in the male-dominant watch industry in Switzerland. Gisele is still based in Switzerland, but her story shows us how women's issues in business are the same the world over. The only way to be successful in a nontraditional business, she demonstrates, is to think outside the box and to put your money where your mouth is and stay the course.

Nancy Underwood is an exporter of environmental services. She has spent countless hours in the classroom to acquire the skills, certifications, and licenses that are necessary to break into the male dominated environmental and safety services arena. An African American woman, she is a shining example of pulling oneself up by the bootstraps—in her case from welfare all the way to the global marketplace. When life dealt her lemons she made lemonade, in part from the recipes she got from her advisors and mentors. Her story underscores the importance of networking, researching, and preparing to go global.

Betsy Haskell is the owner of a hotel in the Republic of Georgia. She is considered a U.S. exporter because she is an American who causes exports to happen. In her case, she actually imports American goods for her hotel into the Republic of Georgia. The author met her on a recent trip to Georgia and interviewed her while there. Many people in the United States know about Betsy, whose fame precedes her because of her bold move to set up a hotel in the Republic of Georgia when the country first declared its independence from the Soviet Union. She clearly wins the prize for doing the most far-out thing—especially since she had never owned her own business, nor did she have any prior hotel experience. Hers is yet another example of the triumph of the spirit.

Geetha Devi is a new exporter of software solutions. She is currently based in Bangalore, India, where her flagship first business, Elmo Lawn Mowers, holds the number one position for sales of lawn mowers in the domestic market of India. Her journey into the world of exporting was also a long and circuitous route and shows us about the power of possibility thinking and about the power of preparation and having a positive and global attitude. She encourages us to prepare ourselves personally and professionally, not only for going global, but also for *being* global in our approach to life.

Margaret Gatti is an international trade lawyer whose law practice counsels firms on how to go global. She provides invaluable advice about how to prepare for going global and shares her insights from her law practice and from her practical experience as an importer and exporter prior to establishing her law practice.

Before further introducing you to the women in this book, it is important to understand the context and status of women business ownership in America.

Women-Owned Business in the U.S. Context

Women-owned businesses are a vital part of our nation's economy. They outpace other small business sectors in growth and participate in every industry. The U.S. Small Business Administration's Office of Advocacy estimates that there were 8.5 million women-owned businesses in 1997, accounting for more than one third of all businesses and generating $3.1 trillion in revenue. Their numbers have been increasing steadily, and more rapidly, than other small businesses in the economy, by 89 percent over the last decade. And their revenues have increased by an astonishing 209 percent over the same period, even after adjusting for inflation. Evidence suggests that women-owned businesses will be even more important to the economy in the new century. The Small Business Administration's Office of Advocacy has also estimated the number and contributions of women-owned businesses in 1997 and made some projections for this year and beyond, as follows:

- Some 23.8 million employees worked for women-owned firms, an increase of 262 percent over the 1987-1997 period.

- More than 1.4 million women-owned businesses with employees generate $2.8 trillion in revenue. The number of women-owned businesses with employees grew by 46 percent from 1987 to 1997.

- Revenue of women-owned businesses with employees grew 221 percent from 1987 to 1997, after adjusting for inflation.

- By the year 2000, it was estimated that women-owned sole proprietorships would number 7.1 million, or 35 percent of all sole proprietorships. The number was expected to grow 33 percent from 1990 to 2000, compared with 23 percent for all sole proprietorships.

- There will be about 4.7 million self-employed women by 2005. This is an increase of 77 percent since 1983, compared with a 6 percent increase in the number of self-employed men.

These data are put into further perspective by understanding the foundations for women's business ownership in America.

A Glimpse into the Past: The Role Women Played in the Colonial Economy

In colonial times, according to Temple University researchers, "everything indicated that, should the need arise, there was nothing in the social or economic code of the times to prevent a woman's supporting herself and her family in whatever way she best could." As far as general business went, women were found buying and selling, suing and being sued, acting as administrators and executors, and having power of attorney. Besides farmers and housewives, colonial women were innkeepers, "she-merchants," artificers, health care providers, teachers, landed proprietors, writers, and printers. Women were also shipbuilders, tailors, shoemakers, bakers, brewers, painters, gilders, and wallpaper hangers, among other occupations.

Colonial women most often made a living in occupations that stressed their traditional female roles as mothers and housekeepers. But the monetization of even the most feminine of occupations transformed "women's work" into a component of the gendered game of wealth accumulation. Women inn and tavern keepers, for example, had to take money and promissory notes from their customers in order to pay their suppliers. The operation of a public house necessitated the hosting of public functions, especially legal and economic ones. Seamstresses often developed into milliners and fancy seamstresses who resold a stock of value-added goods. Because she-merchants often took over the businesses of deceased husbands, colonial women sold a wide-variety of goods from windows to clothes to wines to groceries. A few women were dry goods importers, the top of the colonial and early she merchants' ladder. Other colonial women traders were furniture dealers, hardware traders, booksellers, druggists, and tobacconists. Some she-merchants specialized in certain goods. Clothing and seeds were favorite areas of concentration. Women came to dominate certain trades in some areas.

The role of the *feme sole trader* is particularly important to understand how women-owned firms were able to continue to evolve, grow, and maintain their independence during colonial times. Feme sole traders, according to Temple University researchers, were married women who avoided coverture (a series of legal restrictions that usually accompanied marriage). Feme sole trader status originated in London merchant custom and was adopted by many American colonies. According to English common law, a feme sole trader was a woman whom "the Law of Nature hath put her under the Obedience of her Husband, and hath submitted her Will to his" though "she wants Free Will as Minors want Judgment." Feme Sole Traders could "sue without her husband" in London, if the City agreed. English law was clear, however, that "every Feme which trades in London is not a Feme Sole Trader. If the husband meddle with the Trade of the wife, for example, then she is not a Feme Sole Trader. However, if the husband be beyond Sea, or becomes Bankrupt, or leaves his Trade, and the wife exercise the same Trade, or they both exercise the same Trade distinctly by themselves, and not meddle the one with the other, the wife is "Sole Merchant or Trader."

Just as in England in 1700, in Philadelphia, the issue of the rights of feme sole traders largely concerned the question of whether they could sue or be sued independently of their husbands. "The main question in cases where the husband lives with the wife, and is in and about the business, seems to be: In what capacity is the husband in and about the business?" In other words, is he his wife's agent, employee, or merely trading in her name? Pennsylvania passed an act relative to feme sole traders in 1718. According to this act, a feme sole trader was a married woman who conducted business on her own, with her husband's permission, but without his aid.

Fast Forward to the 20th Century: Feme Sole Traders Today

Today, there are many feme sole traders who call all the shots in their businesses. Arguably, the contemporary women-owned firms that are at the top of the ladder, just as in Colonial times, are those who engage in exporting. The data show that while not many women-owned firms have risen to the top of this ladder, those that have gotten into exporting have done so in a big way. According to the U.S. Department of Commerce's 1992 edition of *Characteristics of Business Owners*, the last year for which data are available, exporting firms owned by women, while less numerous than those owned by men, export more intensively: 30 percent of women-owned firms exported 50 percent or more of their product, compared with 21.9 percent of firms owned by men. Overall, however, the percentage of export sales attributed to the sales of women-owned business of all employee sizes is less than 2 percent in any single industry division, suggesting that there is clearly room for growth.

Understanding the Factors Driving Export Growth

Historians will look back on the 20th century as the time that ushered in globalization and digitalization. In quantitative terms, the impact of globalization and digitalization can be measured as follows:

- **Impact of globalization**: In 1960, total world exports amounted to $629 billion. By 1995, they had risen to more than $5 trillion.

- **Impact of digitalization**: As of May 1999, 171 million people across the globe had access to the Internet. As this number grows, so does the movement toward providing goods and services through the digital medium.

Continued globalization and digitalization are inevitable and irreversible. In the process, markets are mutating with frightening speed, allowing billions of dollars to be moved with the click of a key. The emergence of these twin and simultaneous phenomena means that no business has a secured domestic market, as its domestic market is now somebody else's export market. Today, the individual firm no longer has a choice about going global; remaining domestic may mean lost opportunities and competition in its own backyard."

Understanding Barriers to Exporting among Small Firms

Despite the positive role digitalization has played in opening up global markets, some barriers to exporting remain. Barriers are not only imposed by external factors but also by market imperfections within our own trade infrastructure and system. Perhaps most important are the barriers that are internal to the firm. These internal barriers prevent the firm from being ready to seize global business opportunities. What are these barriers? According to C. Fred Bergsten of the Institute for International Economics, "The adoption of a new mindset of export orientation by U.S. industry…is required to propel more small firms into exporting." Indeed, many scholars and practitioners have offered their insights over the years about the problem of getting more small firms to export. The following comments indicate the common thinking about the export problem:

■ We can bring the markets to them. This is not a problem…the problem is their capacity to plan. To make them exporters, we must first enter their mentality…. Only then can we open their minds.

■ Many U.S. firms are reluctant to consider export prospects and voluntarily exclude themselves from entering new markets because they perceive exporting as too risky, complicated, and not profitable.

■ SMEs don't export because their owner-managers have neither the time nor the inclination to think about it, not because firms don't know they should export.

■ The most serious barrier to exporting is not a lack of competence; rather, it is a lack of commitment and persistence within the firms themselves.

■ Exporting has less to do with how old a company is or how deep its pockets are than it does with managerial vision about market positioning.

Understanding Barriers to Exporting among Women-Owned Firms

As most women-owned firms are small, many of these observations and barriers to exporting apply to them. The question is whether there are also additional barriers that uniquely constrain today's *feme sole trader.* A recent groundbreaking joint initiative between the governments of the United States and Canada took up the challenge to answer this question and to identify barriers to women exporters. Surveys were administered to U.S. and Canadian women-owned firms that exports. The Canadian survey, conducted under the auspices of Trade Research Coalition (TRC), a public/private-sector consortium established by Minister for International Trade, included 254 Canadian businesswomen. (For more information, visit <www.connectuscanada.com/magog.htm>. The U.S. survey, conducted under the auspices of the U.S. Small Business Administration, by the author of this book, Dr. Sharon T. Freeman, included 160 U.S. businesswomen. (For more information, visit <www.sba.gov/oit> or the Office of Women's Business Ownership web site at <www.sba.gov/womeninbusiness>. Although both surveys investigated a broad range of issues related to the export experience of women and the barriers they face, the main findings from the surveys shed light on the following key issues:

■ **Management experience**. Survey results showed that women exporters tend to have significant management and industry experience prior to engaging in exporting.

- **Export start-up**. Survey results showed that today, women exporters tend to start exporting rather quickly, with many having made their first export sale within the first years of business operations.

- **Distribution channels**. Survey results showed that women exporters use a full range of distribution channels to reach foreign markets. However, the most consistently mentioned approaches are direct exporting and the use of sales intermediaries, such as agents and distributors.

- **Sales and growth**. Survey results showed that exporting is seen as a means of increasing the overall sales of the firms, which in turns leads to increases in the number of employees.

- **Seeking advice**. Survey results showed that a significant number of the surveyed firms rely on their direct business partners for export advice rather than outside sources, such as consultants.

- **Export financing**. Survey results showed that the majority of the surveyed firms relied on internal sources of capital to fund export transactions, such as retained earnings, personal sources, and credit cards.

- **Contacts**. Survey results showed that lack of connections was seen as the main obstacle to exporting, while having good contacts was most frequently cited as a major factor for successful exporters.

Some of the advice that was gleaned from the successful women exporters who participated in the surveys can be summarized as follows:

1. Do your homework.
- Investigate the regulations of exporting, such as NAFTA rules of origin.
- Understand brokerage fees and customs issues.
- Learn how government can assist in export activities.
- Research the size and nature of the market.
- Have a firm pricing strategy established before meeting potential clients.

2. Enlist the help of others.
Solicit input and advice from as many sources as possible:
- Clients.

- Suppliers.
- Trade commissioners.
- Foreign tax revenue services.
- Community economic development personnel.

3. Know your markets.
- Understand cultural differences.
- Quote in local currency.
- Start with a broad sweep of the market and then concentrate on your best prospects.

4. Go for it!
- Don't be afraid—be persistent.
- Take a calculated risk, but only invest as much as you can afford to lose.
- Set your goals and work towards them.

5. Ensure your financial security.
- Understand that exporting is a long-term investment.
- Exporting requires cashflow to finance transactions.
- Exporting requires strong financial management.

6. Meet customers' needs.
- Understand cultural differences.
- Understand what the customer is looking for.
- Exceed customers' expectations.

7. Know your product or service and promote it.
- Understand product or service differences.
- Assess the long-term viability of your product in the international marketplace.

8. Establish your goals and define a strategy.
- Consider what you wish to accomplish in life and in the export relationship.
- Understand clearly the business objectives and strategy.
- Stick with it.

9. Know your production and service capabilities.

- Be ready for potential clients' questions.
- Ensure that you have the production capability to meet demand.

This advice can also be found among the stories of the women in this book. It is counsel that straddles two different phenomena: one has to do with overcoming personal constraints of the business owner, while the other has to do with overcoming management and organizational constraints within the firm to exporting. When we say, for instance, "Go for it," what we are really saying is the business owner should have the personal fortitude and strength to take risks. When we say, on the other hand, establish goals and define a strategy, we are saying that the correct management and organizational infrastructure should be put into place at the firm level to support exporting. This book provides further insights into how some women exporters have overcome both personal and firm-level internal barriers to export successfully.

Now, let's have our conversations with the women exporters in this book.

INTERNATIONAL NEWS

Minority firms and exporting: Where do they stand?

By Sharon T. Freeman, Ph.D.
President, African American Small Business Exporters Association (AASBEA)

"Today the individual firm no longer has a choice about going global; remaining domestic may mean lost opportunities and even competition in its own backyard."

Many U.S. firms are reluctant to consider export prospects and voluntarily exclude themselves from entering new markets because they perceive exporting as too risky, complicated and not profitable. Others are simply indifferent to exporting and not willing to invest management time and money. Other firms do not think of exporting because they are not hungry enough. Where do minority firms stand — are they not hungry enough, are they indifferent to exporting, are they not willing to invest the time and money? How much of the potential of minority firms remains untapped? The short answer is: we do not know!

What we do know, however, is that the primary barriers to exporting among smaller businesses as a whole tend to be internal to firms, not external to markets. The key is willingness; firms have to want to export; they have to understand that over 90 percent of the world's consumers are in fact in foreign markets. In order to be successful, however, firms also have to understand that export development is part of a company's development; it is a process, not an event. Experience has shown that successful exporting has less to do with how old a company is or how deep its pockets are than it does with managerial vision about market positioning. Successful companies integrate exporting into the heart of their corporate plan right from the start.

For minority-owned firms that have a vision about how "going global" can be integrated into an overall strategy to enhance their market position, it is imperative that they choose their markets and not let markets choose them. In today's "E-dominated" business environment, the chances of a firm becoming an accidental exporter are quite high. In such cases, exports are a result of an accidental foreign order, not a company strategy. The cost of such adventurism can be quite high.

To overcome adventurism and help firms think strategically about their export options, the Minority Business Development Agency (MBDA) has recently produced a new guide that readers are strongly encouraged to obtain. The MBDA's *Minority Exporters: A Resource Guide '99* provides valuable information to help firms navigate through the maze of export assistance programs to show them the critical path for finding the right markets and the right strategic partners so they can be successful in exporting and grow as a result. Readers are also encouraged to visit MBDA's Virtual International Trade Center at http://www.mbda.gov for information about going global.

Dr. Sharon T. Freeman, president of the newly formed African American Small Business Exporters Association (AASBEA) in Washington, D.C., holds undergraduate and graduate degrees from Carnegie-Mellon University in Pittsburgh. She was awarded a Ph.D. in applied management and decision sciences from Walden University, the nation's premier distance learning graduate program. She is an adjunct professor of international business and export and import management at American University in the Kogod School of Business.

A leading international business development expert, she was appointed as an advisor to the Secretary of Commerce and the U.S. Trade Representative on Small and Minority Business starting in 1993; she is the first vice chair of this committee today. Freeman also serves as a private sector advisor to the State Department and has been elected to serve on the Washington/ Maryland District Export Council (DEC).

Freeman and her colleagues in Lark-Horton, AASBEA and the Foundation are dedicated to helping firms and entities that have been traditionally left out of the globalization loop find new and rewarding critical paths for becoming players in the game. Dr. Freeman and her team of economists, industry experts, infrastructure analysts, and business partners can be reached as follows:

Dr. Sharon T. Freeman

African American Small Business Exporters Association (AASBEA), 2300 M St., NW, Suite 800, Washington, DC 20037. Phone (202) 332-5137, Fax (202) 332-5286, E-mail: LARKHOR@EROLS. COM, Web(s): LarkHorton.com and AASBEA.com.

Dr. Sharon T. Freeman

President

Lark-Horton Global Consulting Limited

and the

All American Small Business Exporters Association, Inc. (AASBEA)

Contact:

AASBEA

2300 M Street, NW, Suite 800
Washington, DC 20037

Phone: (202) 332-5137
Fax: (202) 332-5286
Email: aasbea@aol.com
Web: http://www.aasbea.com

Order on-line at:

http:// www.aasbea.com

Sharon Freeman, Ph.D.
President, Lark-Horton Global Consulting
and the
All American Small Business Exporters Association, Inc.
(AASBEA)

My Dream: The Road Taken

I first traveled to Hong Kong in 1979. At that time, there wasn't much publicity or "buzz" about what was happening there. The only imagery I, and many Americans had, of Hong Kong was the impression left by the old "Suzie Wong" movies of the early 1960s; it was an image of an overcrowded maze of people in falling down shacks with huddled masses yearning to be free. Who knew that those shacks had become glorious feats of architecture or that those huddled masses had huddled together and saved all of their money and had become free? You can imagine my shock and amazement therefore when I pulled up in a taxi to the Regent Hotel on my first night in Hong Kong and saw more Rolls Royces in one instant than I had previously seen in the entire world put together. When I sat in the lobby and watched the ease with which the rich and powerful Chinese people switched in their conversations from Chinese to English as they talked on phones to conduct business while simultaneously dining, I knew that something special was happening in this country and that its secret would soon be revealed to the world. I also knew that I had to be a part of this thrilling and unique economic development success story in history.

On my second day in Hong Kong I went over to the U.S. Consulate and asked the Consul General to give me an introduction to some of the successful American business owners who were operating in Hong Kong. The then Consul General, Burton Levin, said that the one person I needed to meet was Ira Dan Kaye. He was the owner of Lark International, a highly successful garment manufacturing and trading company, established in Hong Kong over 20 years previously, which was arguably the most successful American owned business in Asia at that time. When I met Mr.

Kaye in his majestic office overlooking the Hong Kong harbor on the Kowloon side, I asked him to tell me the secret: "How did you know over 20 years ago that Hong Kong would be so successful and that it would be the place to live?" He said one thing that changed my life: *"Hong Kong is the only place where you can conceive of an idea at 9am, incorporate it at noon, and make your first profit by 5pm."* From that moment forward, every fiber of my being was committed to moving to Hong Kong. I did not know how I was going to do it, and indeed, I had never thought of doing it, but I was hooked and I was going to do it come hell or high water!

The funny thing is that I already had the dream to move overseas before I visited Hong Kong but it never occurred to me to move to Asia. I was a government official at the time and had put a lot of energy into preparing to move to Tunisia. I had studied French at the State Department's Foreign Institute for over one year and had lined up all of my ducks in a row to be stationed with the then U.S. Trade and Development Program (TDP) to Tunis, Tunisia. My dream was to be fluent in French so that one day I could move to Paris and be a part of what I thought was the "high life." I wanted to be a *bon vivant* and sit at dinner in a restaurant and switch between English and French as people attended to me as the world looked on. Europe, to me, was the top of the heap—you really made it if you made it to Paris. What I saw in Hong Kong, however, showed me that while Europe was great, much of its glory was behind it while in the much further and distance land of Hong Kong there was Shangri-La, where its future was in front of it. Robert Frost's poem so elegantly captures my sentiment, my revelation, and my future when he said that —*"two roads diverged in a wood, and I—I took the one less traveled by, and that has made all of the difference."*

Getting to Hong Kong

To say that I had to move mountains to get to Hong Kong is an understatement. First, I had to divorce my husband. Secondly, I had to convince my boss to let me be the Regional Director for Asia of the U.S. Trade and Development Program (TDP) stationed in Hong Kong. This was a hard sell for many reasons; first and foremost, because I played a critical part in managing the day-to-day operations of TDP back in Washington as the Assistant Director of the agency, my departure to Hong Kong would be disruptive for the organization. Unspoken, but perhaps just as important, was the fact that because I was so young, 27 years old, and Black, there was concern about whether I would be totally accepted in the position of Regional Director for Asia. I had to persuade my boss that assigning me to Hong Kong would be in his interest in the long run. Over the next year he gradually became persuaded as he watched me work throughout Asia during our many trips there together.

In particular, he observed two things that won him over to my side, the first was that the Asians embraced me and had empathy for me as a minority, and the second was that I worked as hard as a human being could to market the feasibility study grants that TDP was offering to the Asian nations. After convincing my boss to let me go to Hong Kong, my next hurdle was to convince the State Department's personnel department to induct me into the Foreign Service so that I could be stationed overseas. To make a long story short, I worked it out slowly but surely and by 1981, I moved to Hong Kong!

What I did as TDP's Regional Director for Asia helped to form the foundation for my subsequent consulting business. In brief, my job was to understand the development priorities of each Asian country and to meet with senior officials in different ministries in each country to work out the arrangements to receive TDP grants for the feasibility study of various development projects like airports, telecommunications systems, and other projects. While flying to the different countries in Asia was very glamorous on the one hand, it was enormously hard work at the same time. My life consisted of going to one country after the next without a break in between in order to meet the time pressures we were under to obligate our funds each year. For instance, I would go to China on Sunday, stay for a week, and return to Hong Kong for one day. Then I'd fly to India for a week and return to Hong Kong for one day; next, I'd go to Thailand, the Philippines, Indonesia, Burma, Pakistan, or Korea, and in turn, to each country in Asia where there was a possibility for TDP to provide funds for a feasibility study of a major development project. The vast distances between some of these countries made the travel schedule very arduous. For instance, it takes over five hours to fly to Japan from Hong Kong, and over eight to fly to Papua New Guinea. An adventure was waiting in each country, sometimes the adventure was good, and sometimes it was bad. The good part was that I met wonderful people, on the down side, I spent as many days being sick as I did being well, and as much time trying to locate my luggage as conducting my real business. Aside from these challenges, there was also the stress of not exactly knowing what I was doing. As a non-engineer, the learning curve about how to structure studies for airports, or port development projects was enormous. As I was the only representative of the agency in Hong Kong, I had no one with whom to confer. It was entirely up to me, therefore, to figure where to go, how to get there, whom to meet, and what to talk about while there. So, in between flying around and making all of the necessary time adjustments and food intake adjustments, I also had to stay up at night to read and learn about the actual projects I was supposed to be talking about in each country. Believe me, if I was not as young as I was, I could not have done as much. Of the approximate $25 million the agency had to spend each year, my projects in Asia absorbed no less than 50 percent of the entire budget. Considering that each study involved a grant of less than $250,000, it took a lot of hustling each year to spend all of this money in such small amounts. I did this for five years straight, and I traveled back to TDP headquarters in the U.S. every two months as well.

What I gained from this experience was the knowledge that I had an enormous capacity for work and the ability to figure things out in a short period of time. I also made a lot of contacts throughout Asia and developed a deep understanding of how the economies of the different Asian nations operated. This knowledge and background gave me the confidence to establish my consulting business in Hong Kong in 1985.

Having something to sell

After all that I had been through, I figured that I had something to sell! Simply put, I wanted to sell my knowledge of the countries, of the key decisionmakers, and of how to figure things out. While on the one hand this sounds straightforward, on the other, it is not. It goes to the very heart of the question about *what is a consultant?*

Essentially, consultants are "craft entrepreneurs." However, unlike that of "craft entrepreneurs," such as dressmakers, caterers, and others who have well-defined skills and well-defined markets for their crafts, the skills and markets of consultants are not so clearly defined.

This reality was driven home when I asked my colleague, with whom I had worked at TDP and with whom I had traveled all over the world, to join me in my new consulting business and I got his response. Despite the fact that we had traveled the same roads, our roads diverged somewhere along the path; he could not imagine that we knew enough or fit the profile of consultants, especially in my case, as I was Black woman.

My colleague was not the only one who had reservations about my establishing a consulting business in Hong Kong. In fact, my biggest challenge was managing everyone else's fear and concern for me. Frankly, everybody thought I was crazy to start my own business in Hong Kong, in part because they weren't sure if I could succeed, and in part, because they knew that I'd be giving up the many advantages I had that were tied to my employment in the U.S. government. One of my Chinese girlfriends, who was also in the U.S. Diplomatic Service in Hong Kong, itemized what I'd be giving up in this way: "You have a beautiful apartment, a chauffeur, an unlimited travel budget, a Diplomatic Passport, and you are your own boss—-how can you give this up?" Many others were concerned for me because I was Black: they did not believe that anyone would hire a Black woman to help them market in Asia. In fact, the list of concerns about my ability to "make it" was endless: concern for me because I was a Black woman; concern for me because I was young—when Asians respected older age; concern for because I was not married; concern for me because I was an American in Asia, and so forth. Yes, I heard this, and maybe they were all correct, but I had to do it anyway and I had to see for myself. I always believed that my assets would outweigh these considerations. In fact, nobody thought I was doing the right thing but Ira Dan Kaye, of Lark International, who became my partner.

The bottom line is that I could withstand the pressure of everybody else's fear because, in my view, I had something to sell!

Furthermore, when I looked back on my life, I realized that I had always been on an unusual journey on a *road not commonly taken*. In the early 1970s I started out as the sole Black undergraduate in my discipline (cognitive psychology) at Carnegie-Mellon University; later, I became the sole Black female consultant in the division in which I worked at Booz, Allen, & Hamilton; and subsequently, I became the sole Black senior-ranking official at the U.S. Consulate in Hong Kong. Because being a minority was a familiar state of being, I had long ago learned how to rely on myself, how to listen to my own voice, and how to stand alone.

As for my own assessment of my risk, it was quite simple: I knew exactly how much money I was going to devote to my new consulting venture. If that ran out before I could make any more, I'd simply go back home and rejoin the ranks of the employed. My risks were measured in strictly quantitative terms, not in emotional terms. I figured I could not lose in the broader scheme of things, as I would have gained invaluable experience and further personal strength for having had the nerve to do it.

Building and nurturing self confidence...

There are many sources of self-confidence, and many ways in which self-confidence plays a role in business success. On a personal level, I felt confident about myself. I felt confident about my intelligence, about my educational background and preparation, about my appearance, and about my quotient of inner personal strength. It is my inner strength that has enabled me to dig my heels in, look any potential client in the eye, and not blink under any circumstances. One of the most important sources of strength I possessed, and one of the factors that helped me in business negotiations, was the fact that I was not afraid of men. As all of my clients were men, I had to be able to approach them with confidence and make them feel comfortable in the process.

In fact, the importance of making male clients feel comfortable cannot be overstated. I'll never forget going to lunch with a potential male client in Hong Kong. As soon as we sat down, he said, "Jesus, I hope that you can actually eat some food and are not going to sit here and tell me what you cannot eat!" He wanted the experience of having lunch with me to feel the same as that of sitting down with a male colleague over lunch. Fortunately, I had always had extremely positive relationships with men, starting with my father, continuing with my childhood male friends, and throughout my adult life. As a result, I did not harbor any negative feelings about men, nor did I assume that they wanted to shut me out of the game. In short, I went into every business situation with men feeling positive and strong. My male clients perceived this and believed that if they did business with me, it would not feel that different from doing business with men.

Just as having positive work relationships with men can help to build confidence, having positive relationships with women can do the same. In my case, I had a very strong and positive role model in my mother, an entrepreneur who mastered a difficult and segregated business environment in Philadelphia starting in the early 1940s. She was a "target of opportunity entrepreneur" who engaged in many forms of business, from real estate, to insurance, to cosmetics, among others. The whole family got involved in these different businesses. My siblings and I helped out in my parents cosmetic business by helping to pack and label cosmetic jars on the weekends. It was very exciting and gave me the impression that all things were possible. There was no fear associated with business in my household or ever in my mind.

From a business point of view, I felt confident about possessing the requisite experience, skills, knowledge, and contacts to be an effective consultant in Asia. The challenge for me was not whether I had self-confidence; rather, my challenge was to help others have the same level of confidence in me that I had in myself. The key to my success in this was preparation—doing my homework. Before I approached a client, I knew what I was selling and could clearly articulate why the client should buy it. The foundation for this was having undertaken in-depth research on my target clients and on the factors of the business situation I was promoting. The better I did this, the more successful I was. When I was not successful, it was generally not because of an inadequate level of preparation on my part; rather, it was usually because of other factors that did not permit the firm to proceed. In this regard, one of the most important lessons I had to learn was how to distinguish the failure to win the job from a feeling of personal failure. This was not always easy to do in the beginning. When I won an assignment I certainly associated that win with myself. By contrast, I did not want to associate the loss to myself. Over the years it has become easier to handle defeat. I have learned that everything comes around again. All I have to do is keep my proposals in a drawer, and years later somebody else will buy them—"wins" are only postponed.

Having some fear is only natural, however...

As going global and starting my first business occurred simultaneously, I certainly had some justifiable fears and concerns about the process. Yes, I knew I had something to sell but this does not mean that I thought I knew exactly how to sell it or how the manage a business as a first time business owner. My initial concerns had more to do with the process of how to set up and manage a business than about how to get the business. While the prospect of setting my first company up under the British system of law that prevailed in Hong Kong was somewhat daunting, my main concern was about being sued for something. Although the ability to be sued in one's own name was considered an accomplishment for *feme sole traders* in colonial times, I did not view it as a privilege in my case. I didn't know who would sue me for what, but I was afraid nevertheless. My fears were justified when I was sued on my very first day of business.

A real estate agency that claimed that I failed to pay the agency fee for finding me an apartment in Hong Kong brought a suit against me. In fact, I asked the agency to get me into a certain apartment on November 1, 1985, but it failed to do so. I then approached the owner of the apartment directly and worked out my own deal for getting an apartment in the building. When the real estate agency found out I had moved into the building, it demanded an agent's finders fee from me. I ignored all of their threatening correspondence until one day I saw something particularly threatening, opened it, and realized that I had an obligation to pay unless I did something. So I hired a lawyer to argue my case. The lawyer failed to do so to my satisfaction, so I fired the lawyer and handled my own case. I did not get off to a good start as my own lawyer. The first event was a trial in a judge's chambers, which I though was the actual trial to argue the case. In fact, this was not *the* trial. Rather, it was a hearing to allocate court costs.

The judge asked whether I agreed that the "costs be to the plaintiff." I said, "Absolutely"—thinking that this statement meant that the plaintiff would pay the costs; instead, it meant that I would pay the costs. In error, I had agreed to pay all of the court costs.

Finally we had the actual court trial, where the plaintiff had both a barrister and a solicitor. They read verbatim from law books, establishing that the agent and I had a contract. I, however, did not dispute that we had a contract. My issue was that the agency had not lived up to its responsibilities under the contract. When it was finally my turn to address the court, I said I had only one thing to say: *Our contract stated that the agency would find the apartment on November 1, 1985 and it did not do that—-I rest my case.* I won!

Through this episode I came face to face with my greatest fear and prevailed. Whenever this happens, one is empowered! Winning that suit showed me that I had the power to manage my fears and to determine outcomes based on pure and simple logic. This realization has enabled me to approach difficult assignments in my consulting business with confidence in the knowledge that things can be figured out, even if they are in a different language, in a different country, and when I had no prior experience in the realm.

Planning my global business...

It took me two years from the time I conceived the business idea to establish the business. It was important to have a clear conception of what I wanted to sell, of my target clients were, and of what resources I needed in order to sell my services. In view of the latter, I considered whether I needed a strategic partner to help position me in the business.

Having worked throughout Asia and having formed good relationships with many important and powerful people, I believed that I had a lot of good candidates with whom to partner. In the final assessment, I decided that partnering would be beneficial, though not necessarily essential. My number one choice for a partner was chosen, in the main, because the firm's owner was, to be frank, extremely handsome. Fortunately, in the end, my better judgment prevailed and I decided to go with a different partner. This partner chose me. He was Ira Dan Kaye, the first person I met in Hong Kong back in 1979. By 1985, he owned many businesses, but his flagship business was still apparel marketing and manufacturing. He had the vision to set up in Hong Kong to supply other retail stores in the United States before there were any apparel quota restrictions (quantitative limits on the amount of the goods that could be shipped into the U.S. from supplying countries). When quotas were imposed, Ira was granted a large quota holding. With that, he set up manufacturing and representative offices throughout Asia. He heard me speak at an American Chamber of Commerce function one day and told me that, when I was ready, I should leave the U.S. government and join him to make some real money. The "real money" part sounded intriguing and I said, "What are we going to call our new business partnership?"

His firm was Lark International, and my newly incorporated firm was called "S.F. Horton & Associates." (Horton being my previous married name that I still used at the time). So we named our joint venture Lark-Horton Connections.

It is important to explain what my expectations were of my partner and vice versa. What I really wanted was a big name behind me. Yes, I did have confidence in myself, but that does not mean that bigger was not better. And to be really honest, although I was mentally prepared to go into this business entirely on my own, it provided an additional comfort level to have a rich White man back behind me. I also thought that this would provide an additional comfort factor for my clients. When they chose our firm, they would be comforted in knowing that they had chosen a large firm to undertake their work.

On balance, having a joint venture partner did indeed provide the security blanket I needed. While I was responsible for making my own money within our partnership, I felt that I had someone behind me. Moreover, because our consulting practice was operated out of Lark's prestigious offices in Kowloon, Hong Kong, I could always proudly hold my head high when corporate visitors came to call. I felt "big" and felt that I was apart of something even bigger through Lark International. Having a partner also motivated and drove me to work even harder because I wanted to prove to him that he had chosen the right person. To this day, 15 years later, I think of him with every accomplishment, taking a moment to ask him in my heart if he is proud of me. Although Ira died in July 1999, he will always be with me.

Through our partnership, Ira sought an opportunity to help someone who he believed to be worthy of his attention. He did not need me or any money associated with our consulting firm operation; rather, he liked the buzz of having a young person come into his organization with fresh ideas and abundant energy. Many years later, one of his long-term staff members asked me, "Why does Ira value the little small money you make in the consulting firm more highly than he values all of the money I save him as an accountant?" The answer was that Ira liked new money. All the accountant was doing was managing money that Ira had already made.

While having a partner helped boost my confidence, it did not necessarily boost my bank account. It was up to me to figure this business out.

The key to planning my global business was as much my attitude as my preparation. My preparation helped me to identify target clients and to plan what to do and how to do it. But it was my attitude that prepared me to handle the actual situations that occurred. And it was a good thing that I had the right mental attitude because I needed it! As it turns out, while I had a long list of probable clients and many verbal commitments to hire my firm once it was established, I did not get a single one of those contracts I thought I was going to get. All of those "guys" from the big U.S. corporations who told me they were going to give me a contract flat out lied, and I had to start from scratch. Every assignment I eventually won was a result of cold calling. To get started, I flew back to America and and visited various firms. I remembered visiting the President of U.S. Steel and going to dinner with him in Pittsburgh and having him give me a positive indication that he would hire me to help them develop their business in China. It would have been a real feather in my cap to get that assignment because it was U.S. Steel and they were in Pittsburgh where I had gone to and struggled at Carnegie-Mellon; it would have been a little victory to land one of the biggest firms in Pittsburgh. But alas, he lied and I did not get the job—this happened many times, by the way. Fortunately, it did not happen with Soros Associates, which at the time was one of America's leading port development firms. I was able to get an appointment to meet the President of the firm, Paul Soros (brother of famous George Soros). I asked him straight out to hire my firm, Lark-Horton Connections, to represent Soros in Asia. He asked me equally straight out why he should do that, and I told him it was because I would make him money. He responded, "You are hired!" I am happy to say that 15 years later, we are still working together.

In general, the process of identifying clients entailed two aspects: understanding the demand side of the equation—knowing where the business was for U.S. clients in respect to major projects in Asia, and, secondly, knowing which U.S. firms had the requisite qualifications to bid on the different project opportunities. Today, with access to the Internet, this does not seem a daunting challenge, but undertaking such research from Hong Kong prior to the Internet was difficult. Furthermore, prior to the widespread use of facsimile machines and later email, it was also expensive to communicate between countries. We relied on telexes and cables, which were very expensive and cumbersome. Under these circumstances, we wanted to be sure that the potential client was a good candidate and that our cold calling was not really "cold." We spent a lot of time in commercial libraries undertaking research on the U.S. companies we wanted to approach before we approached them, because once we opened the line of communication with a firm, it started getting very expensive very quickly.

The expense of doing business under these circumstances also had major implications for our later import-export business trials. Just to give you a glimpse of what was involved: I would get an inquiry from a Chinese firm to purchase fertilizer from the United States. I would undertake research in the library to identify which firms to approach, then I would embark upon a nightmare series of telexing back and forth from China, to Hong Kong, to the United States. All of this cost a lot of money. To lower our costs, I had to plan my strategies very well in advance, being sure I had all of the specifications nailed down before I passed on the inquiry. If I did not do this up-front, then I would have to do it while the clock was ticking, so to speak, via a series of expensive telexes and phone calls.

The bottom line is that given the cost of operating from Hong Kong, when I approached a deal or a potential deal, I had to have done my research up-front or else I would waste a lot of time and money ironing out the details on the back end. The need to save money made me develop a discipline about how I approached my work; namely, I had to be careful, thorough, and know how to access many resources for free that helped us lower the costs of doing the job. Research, research, research—that what is was all about then and still is now. As a firm, we distinguish ourselves by the quality of research we undertake and the speed with which we undertake it. Thus, for our clients, it is more cost-efficient to hire us than for them to do it themselves.

Building my global business...

Now that I was in this business, I had to figure out how to grow it. Starting out, I had positioning, knowledge, and the inside track on Asia, but I really didn't have a strategy for growing the business. The truth is I just wanted to be hired by anybody to do anything—but what I really wanted was to be a player and to be in the game. Being an international consultant and operating from Hong Kong was for me the top of the consulting game. You could say that my goals were not really corporate when I started out, they were personal: I wanted to be hired, I wanted to undertake a broad range of challenging assignments in Asia, and I wanted to be prove to everybody that a Black woman could do what I intended to do. More specifically, what I wanted to prove was that if I knew what I was doing that my ethnicity, gender, and relative youth would not be a constraint in my ability to sell my services.

Once I was firmly in the game, I was on my own to chart my course and figure out how to grow. No one provided strategic advice to me, and no one could. What I was trying to do was unprecedented. As I stated earlier, my partner's role was limited to providing emotional and institutional support; it was up to me to figure out how to use his resources. All that my partner said to me was, Go! He provided an enabling environment for me to be all I could be.

While I cannot say that I had specific quantitative objectives for my business growth, I did have a sound strategy for doing my business and the expectation that through doing a job well that my business would grow.

One of my stocks in trade that I cultivated was knowing how to access the information I needed to perform my consulting assignments. Here is how my informational needs typically broke down: First, I needed subject matter data. If, for instance, we were doing a study of the apparel market in China, we needed data on apparel demand, consumption, production, prices, market structure, et cetera. As different organizations within China were the repositories of this information, the trick was to find out which agencies had which data. The next level of difficulty was to ascertain who among our contacts could give us access to the agencies that had the information we sought. After sorting out various internal information sources within China, in this example, the next mission was to identify external information sources about China. A big "win" would be to find studies about the China apparel industry that were performed by the World Bank or by other public or private organizations. The challenge here again was to identify the right organizations and the right people in the organizations who could give us access to the required information.

The U.S. government was often a source of information for many of our assignments. Before we did anything else, we always wanted to know what we could get for free from the U.S. government. We had to know precisely which departments to go to for information; this entailed undertaking a great deal of research (prior to the Internet) to pinpoint our sources.

On balance, I could say that cultivating contacts has been one of the most important strategies for growing my business.

Among my contacts, foreign country planning officials have been among the most important, especially in China. The Chinese, for instance, have many networks; therefore knowing one person in one locale could provide me with access to all of that person's contacts in other regions of China. For instance, when I was undertaking a client assignment for the U.S. firm Foster Wheeler, I was traveling in the interior of China. My passport was stolen from my Chinese host who was traveling with it on a bus. I contacted one of my Chinese connections in Beijing, who called the local police force in the city where my passport was stolen. Within 24 hours I had my passport back. Similarly, my contacts would call their friends who were in charge of various departments and agencies in China to encourage them to give me the information I needed. My contacts vouched for me, which made all the difference in my ability to deliver on the client assignment for which I was retained.

On the other side of the equation, it has always been important for me to maintain contact with U.S. firms. While living in Hong Kong, I relied very heavily upon the American Chamber of Commerce (AMCHAM) network throughout Asia to invite me to meetings to meet delegations from the United States. I hosted many of these delegations through AMCHAM, which became a great source of business for my firm.

Having contacts was not my problem, really. Knowing how to effectively use them and how to ensure there was always a fair quid pro quo was the challenge. I always went with my gut feeling: if I felt that I was asking for more then I could repay, I did not ask for the favor. If, on the other hand, I knew how to pay back the favor, then I made sure the person from whom I was seeking the favor was informed about how I intended to repay my debt. The bottom line is that contacts are very important. They have to be kept fresh and they must be rewarded, as there is no such thing as a free lunch.

In addition to the overall issue of developing and managing contacts, I had two other important strategic considerations. One was financing and the other was management.

Regarding financing, when I started my consulting business I did not require access to external capital. I was selling a service, and I had office premises and support services through Lark

International. Had I not had access to these inputs, I was prepared to finance my operations entirely out of my own funds. Had I not been able to obtain consulting contracts my funds would have been exhausted after one year. Fortunately, however, I hit the ground running and was able to get contracts right away. In fact, one of my first was with the Flying Tigers to conduct an air cargo demand study in China. It was a big contract, and it created a business base that I was able to build upon in my consulting practice. Although our firm has been able to finance its operations internally, we were always aware of a broad range of financing options, including those that were available from the U.S. Small Business Administration (SBA), the Export-Import Bank (EXIM), the Overseas Private Investment Company (OPIC), and other sources of capital. Fortunately, we have not had to rely on external financing, although we stay current about new developments in these programs so we can advise our clients about how to tap these resources.

Regarding management, the key issue for me has always been what to control and what to delegate within the context of particular assignments. As our firm's assignments vary considerably from one to the next, it is often necessary to retain new and untried personnel for each assignment. In most cases, this has not worked well. The problem is that many of our assignments are very challenging and in underdeveloped countries. We have found that unless experts are familiar with such situations, they find it difficult to apply their experience in an unfamiliar setting. To give you an example, I hired one of my best friends to conduct a review of the leather sector in Kenya. He did this work all of the time in Italy, but when he came to Kenya and saw how underdeveloped the industry was there he was so overwhelmed by the difference in the situation he could not perform the task. This shows that is not just a person's credentials on paper or even their experience in the field that will make them a good consultant. One must have the right attitude and believe that he can do the job whatever the job is and wherever it is.

Experiences like this have made us reluctant to bid on assignments that require a lot of hired experts. At the same time, as our assignments vary so considerably from one to the next, it is also difficult to retain in-house experts along a broad range of disciplines. Our approach has been to try to be in the driver's seat as much as possible to create our own assignments so we can formulate our team in advance. As a small firm owner whose personal reputation is synonymous with that of the firm, I want to make sure that we perform every job well. In fact, it is only because of our good reputation that we are ever hired. In this regard, I am very much like the other women in this book who so highly value customer satisfaction and who consider it as a measure of success.

The evolution of my consulting practice...

Our first wave of consulting business focused on helping U.S. firms to identify and get involved in major development projects in Asia. Next, we focused on performing indepth market studies for firms that wanted to enter the Asia market to manufacture or distribute their products. Eventually we got into investment promotion to help countries in the Caribbean and Latin America attract investment into their Free Trade Zones from Hong Kong, Taiwan, and Korea. This in turn led to helping countries to figure out how to develop an investment regime that attracted certain manufacturing industries. Our next frontier was designing Free Trade Zones in various countries in Africa and Latin America.

By this time it was 1994 and I had already worked in over 100 countries. It was time for me to return to the U.S. to spend more time with my family. This timeframe coincided with a number of momentous events that had a major impact on our consulting business.

One major development was widespread digitalization. The Internet helped my business in many ways. It provided a low-cost and reliable means of enabling me to communicate with my contacts around the world. Internet access also facilitated my ability to conduct research about the social, economic, and political conditions of the various countries in which my firm works. One of the first things my colleagues and I do, for instance, before we commence an overseas consulting assignment is to refer to the U.S. Department of Commerce's *National Trade Data Bank* which has a wealth of information that we can access at no cost at Federal Depository libraries.

At first, I was worried when the Internet came into prominence; one of my firm's competitive advantages had always been its ability to access information from sources that others could not access. The Internet threatened to give all of our competitors and our clients access to this same information and thereby level the playing field. My fears were quickly allayed, however, when I realized that it takes a lot of discipline to use the Internet properly, a discipline that many do not adhere to when using the Internet. Many users simply download information without taking time to read it or evaluate it. I realized that we would have a new competitive advantage as a kind of "information intermediary": one who actually reads, evaluates, and synthesizes the information.

As it turns out, the Internet is the best thing that ever happened to my consulting business. Instead of making our clients feel that they do not need a consultant, they feel so overwhelmed by all of the information they need a consultant even more.

Widespread democratization has also created new consulting opportunities for our firm because many newly democratizing nations have not yet had an opportunity to develop the appropriate policies, institutions, and infrastructure to support private sector growth. As a consequence, the transition has not been smooth, to put it mildly. The question that my firm is called upon by the World Bank, the U.S. Agency for International Development, the African Development Bank, the Asian Development Bank, the InterAmerican Development Bank, and others to help address is that of what can be done to accelerate the adjustment process when virtually all systems to support such acceleration are either missing or broken.

Widespread globalization, on the other hand, has brought another set of problems that lead to consulting opportunities for our firm. Everybody wants to be in the export game but few can effectively play. In order to compete, firms have to have better *quality*, better *prices*, or better *delivery terms* for their export products than their global competitors. There has been a demand for my firm services to help formulate export development strategies in different countries overseas, especially increasingly in the former Soviet Union.

Then there is the impact of E-commerce and the opportunities it has created for our firm to counsel firms about getting E-commerce enabled and export ready at the same time.

There is no doubt that the world is changing at lightning speed, as a consultant the onus is on me to embrace and master these changes. This calls for constant investments in upgrading my skills and constant research about my target clients and their changing priorities and strategies. My client targets are institutions like the World Bank, the United Nations, the Agency for International Development, and others. Therefore, I must constantly assess and reassess how they are planning to address the challenges of development in the world so that I can demonstrate how my consulting firm is prepared to contribute to helping them meet their goals. In this regard, there are no shortcuts in the research process; I actually have to identify and analyze the strategy papers of these organizations and develop and maintain information about who is in charge of what at the different institutions.

Maintaining balance...

When I first started my global business I was not married. After having had been in business for two years I got married in Hong Kong. While my husband and I had an understanding about the travel required for my business, the unfortunate consequence of so much travel was that when I returned home I owed him all of my time. This sliced my life into only two parts, the job and the husband. There was no time for other friends and other pursuits. I felt guilty for doing anything that wasn't focused on my husband during my brief stays at home. In the end—and the marriage did end—I felt like I was a prisoner. In retrospect, I realize that I did not develop a multifaceted social life. Having learned my lesson, I now carve out my time for myself, and I put more effort into joining more business organizations that enable me to pursue broader interests.

My personal story is similar to that of the other women profiled in this book: Once we stopped standing alone and made more times for friends and broadened our circles, we all became happier people.

The women in the book also speak to the issue of how to conduct themselves while working overseas. The common message from all of us is that it is important to conduct business during business hours and to avoid any possibility that work relationships could extend to personal relationships. One final observation that is again common to all of the stories in this book is that it is critical for women to maintain their physical discipline, just as we strengthen our mental discipline. What we have all learned is that in order to be chosen, people have to want to know you. And they will not want to know you if you do not appear to have yourself together. This is particularly important for sellers of consulting services, like myself, who are selling their vision and wisdom. Being out of shape physically may leave the impression that one is not in total control of oneself. More importantly, taking charge of one's physical self is as important a foundation for self-confidence as intellectual prowess.

One funny story that I can share, speaking of appearances, is from one of my assignments in Kenya. My Kenyan client, the head of a Kenyan government agency, and I were riding in the special elevator to meet the vice president of the country. My client, a tall, very rotund man, looked down on me and said, "Sharon, I thought you were going to wear your high heels today." I said that I had them on already.

At only five feet tall, I am still very short even in high heels. For one moment my client wished that I were bigger so it would look like he had a "big consultant." Appearances clearly do matter— but they matter in a non-obvious way: in terms of giving the appearance of power, control, and discipline. So even at five feet, you can look big *most of the time* and be remembered as being even bigger. Every time I meet someone I know, they said that I have lost weight. The reason is they remember as being bigger!

Here is hoping that all women who go global leave a big impression!

*   *   *

A comprehensive guide for export planning is provided in the Appendix.

I invite you to join my export association, the **All American Small Business Exporters Association (AASBEA)** to obtain up-to-date information, publications, and advice about exporting.

Please visit our website at: **http://www.AASBEA.COM**

Maria de Lourdes Sobrino
  President and CEO
  LuLu's Dessert
  and
  Fancy Fruit

Contact:

LuLu's Dessert
5452 Oceanus Drive
Huntington Beach, California 92649

Phone: (714) 895-5483
Fax: (714) 373-2350
Email: mariasobrino@lulusdessert.com
Web: http://www.LuLuusdessert.com

BEATING THE ODDS
BY MICHELLE PRATHER

Gettin' Jiggly With It

Entering a market dominated by a certain hyphenated superbrand and Bill Cosby's mug is no picnic.

Bring up the subject of Mexican immigrants living in poverty, and Maria de Lourdes Sobrino will step onto her soap box and give you a thoughtful lecture. Understand, this relentless woman doesn't believe in being a victim and never has. And in her 47 years, Sobrino has never considered a move so weak. She's gone from making her family proud to making their jaws drop in disbelief. She's been cut off from her first husband and their daughter, and gone into multiple-year debt, all in pursuit of the American dream she feels so many take for granted.

You'd think it was a Lifetime drama series, but these are merely snapshots of Sobrino's rise to president and CEO of LuLu's Dessert Factory in Huntington Beach, California. Unlike the ready-to-eat snacks that Sobrino produces, her success didn't come perfectly packaged. But it did come from scratch.

"My family in Mexico calls me the adventurer," says Sobrino, a woman whose smile doesn't reflect the hurt she felt when relatives scoffed at some of the choices she made. Not only did Sobrino stay in the United States after she opened a Los Angeles branch of her Mexico City-based travel and convention management company in 1981, but she also chose to start a gelatin company when the travel business went the way of the peso in 1982. " 'Gelatina?' they'd say," recalls Sobrino. "It was like my family was a bit ashamed of me after being a business administrator and in the tourism business."

But don't be fooled. The eldest of five children strayed from the pack long before she built a $9.2 million business based on the gigantic, wiggly ring-molds her mother had made for social gatherings in Mexico. Although the culture in Mexico dictated that children follow their parents' career paths, writing depositions and researching case studies didn't appeal to Sobrino, daughter of an attorney and relative to many more. Instead, amidst earning degrees in accounting and business administration, she opened a flower shop in a nearby hotel, and then another after marrying at 21.

But peddling flora wasn't getting Sobrino any closer to her true goal. "My dream since I was very young was to live in the United States," she says. Leaving floristry behind to start a travel and convention firm handling corporate accounts in San Francisco, Miami and Las Vegas seemed just the ticket.

CALIFORNIA DREAMING

By 1981, Sobrino, her husband and their young daughter had transplanted to Los Angeles to open the second office of Mexico & Westside Connection Corp. But 1982 saw both the incorporation and demise of the travel business after the devaluation of the peso devastated Mexico. "It stopped my business completely," says Sobrino.

Her business wasn't all that stopped. Due to a deteriorating relationship and the struggle to raise a 7-year-old daughter at the height of a recession, Sobrino's marriage also halted. Her daughter and now-ex-husband retreated south, but Sobrino remained. "I believed it was a good opportunity," she says, "and I was afraid to go back to Mexico because I thought things there were going to change a lot. And they did."

Attempting to find a strategy for survival, Sobrino sold property she had in Mexico and lived off the money. "I even

HAVE A CUP: *Maria de Lourdes Sobrino knew ready-to-eat gelatin was ready-to-sell. Consumers needed convincing.*

"I'll Take Those Odds."

No business is a guaranteed success. As an entrepreneur, you face not only financial peril, but stress that would put most 9-to-5ers out of business—and not all of you make it. Of course, the greater the odds, the greater the payoff, and these are the stories of those of you who prove it.

THE MATCHUP

The Ent: VS. The Odds

Since she was a 1st, Maria de Lourdes Sobrino saw red, white and blue when she dreamed big. Bringing with her an indomitable spirit, entrepreneurial dreams and a product from her native Mexico that couldn't be found in U.S. markets, she knew she could find a niche.

Sobrino was launching an untried product—ready-to-eat gelatin—that even giant Jell-O wouldn't attempt for another 10 years. Family and consumers alike had no idea what she was trying to do, and a roller coaster of debt nearly added her to the business failure rate.

"At the beginning, my family in Mexico really felt I was crazy." —*Maria de Lourdes Sobrino*

THE OUTCOME

LuLu's Dessert Factory, a favorite in large grocery chains, grossed $9.2 million last year and predicts $12 million in 2000 and $30 million by 2002.

JANUARY 2000   ENTREPRENEUR 143

Maria Sorbino
President and CEO, LuLu's Dessert

Sharon: *Maria, when I read the article in Entrepreneur about you, I was so moved and so impressed but your accomplishments. Furthermore, when I met you and found you to be such a warm and lovely person who is so interested in learning and growing, I knew that I had to get you to tell our audience your story. I am so glad that you are willing to share your experiences with us so that we may all learn from your success. Indeed, how many women in America win the U.S. Small Business Administration's Entrepreneur of the Year award, as you recently have—and how many women are able to grow their businesses to a multimillion dollar enterprise virtually single handedly? Not only have you conquered America against all the odds and in the face of much adversity, but you also have plans to conquer the world. Please tell us how you did it and the secrets to your success.*

Maria: My life as an entrepreneur began in 1976. My first business was in the tourism industry, in Mexico. My initial focus was on organizing conventions and events. I struck upon this idea because I was previously working in conventions management for one of the largest hotels in Mexico City. Over the years, I noticed that our hotel's customers did not want to come back to the same hotel every year; instead, they wanted to stay at the newest hotel or they wanted to have a convention in Cancun. So, in order to meet this demand I decided to put together a "groups and convention company" to place customers in any hotel of their choice throughout Mexico.

Sharon: *How did it feel to going into business? Was it invigorating?*

Maria: Indeed, I found the entrepreneur in myself that I didn't even know was there, and it was exhilarating. I was pregnant, I remember, with my first child when I organized my first international convention in Cancun. It was at a time when President Echeverria officially inaugurated Cancun. There was a lot of fanfare, and many presidents from around the world attended. No expense was spared in planning the event. I had access to a private airplane and to whatever resources I needed to make it happen. It was exciting, and I felt like I would soon be giving birth not only to my new baby but also to my new business and to my new way of life as an entrepreneur.

Sharon: *How did you penetrate the U.S. market?*

Maria: My strategy was to develop a client base from among the large American corporations based in Mexico that regularly had conventions and seminars in Mexico. I arranged the conventions for such companies as IBM, Xerox, Stanhome, Bancomer Avon, and others. I was paid on a commission basis by the hotels, and it was a very, very good business. This way of doing business was also good for the hotels, as they did not have to maintain a public relations department. It was a win-win situation. Eventually, my business expanded, as I added a few flower shops to service both my convention business and my special events planning business.

Sharon: *How did you get the big companies to do business with you? Did you cold call your potential American clients that were based in Mexico, or did they come to you?*

Maria: Most of my target clients had met me before when I was in charge of the conventions departments of the Fiesta Palace and Del Prado Hotels. Many of my clients solicited my services to plan their future conventions at newer hotels in Mexico. In order to meet this demand I had to go out on my own.

Sharon: *So, in a nutshell, the convention planning business opportunity presented itself.*

Maria: Yes, the business found me. Once found, I immediately saw its potential. My only concern was that I did not want to be disloyal to my previous employer. However, we found a way to continue to work together. I placed as many conventions with them as possible, and in return, they paid me a commission directly from the hotel. So, again, it was a win-win situation.

Sharon: *At this point you have a convention planning business, and a flower shop concession. Were there any other components of your business?*

Maria: Yes, I added a travel agency and eventually began to arrange conventions in the United States for my Mexican clientele. My convention business in the United States was focused on Miami, then later on Los Angeles, San Antonio, and Las Vegas. At the time, the exchange rate of the Mexican peso to the U.S. dollar was favorable to my Mexican clientele.

Sharon: *So through planning conventions in the U.S. you came to know America pretty well.*

Maria: Not really. My travel was limited in the United States to those cities in which I was planning events. And my exposure to those cities was limited to the scope of my convention business.

Sharon: *What came next in your business growth?*

Maria: I expanded our conventions business in the United States to a full service holiday package service. Our packages, for such hotels as Caesar's Palace, included airline tickets, hotels, and an entertainment package. We had up to 500 different customers at one time for places like Las Vegas. As I analyzed how my customers were using their entertainment packages something dawned on me: while many of them paid to attend shows, for instance, in Las Vegas, they did not show up and gambled instead. In the end, I realized that I only had to actually pay in advance for 50 percent of the seats I sold to my clients on a pre-paid basis, betting that at least half of them would not show up. So, gradually I learned ways of increasing our profit margin. As business was going so well in the United

States, I decided to open an office in Los Angeles at the Sheraton Plaza La Reina near the Los Angeles airport in 1982.

Sharon: *Does this mean that you decided to live in the United States, or was it your intention to have someone else operate the company in the United States?*

Maria: I was planning to come to United States to operate the company because it had always my dream to do so.

Sharon: *Didn't you say that you had a child? So weren't your married, and if so, how did this decision impact your husband?*

Maria: I was divorced already by this time. However, the story of our marriage does not end here. We worked out a visitation program for our daughter that required my former husband to travel back and forth from Mexico to the United States. Over time, we decided to give our marriage another try. My husband moved to the States, but when it did not work after a few years, he returned to Mexico with our daughter.

Sharon: *How did you work out your immigration situation here in America?*

Maria: I hired an attorney to prepare my immigration documents. I was applying as an investor and was successful in obtaining an L1 visa. I finally became a U.S. citizen about three years ago. I am proud that I did the whole thing on my own. I did not take any shortcuts, like marrying an American. I simply waited my time and went through the official procedures.

Sharon: *Immigrating to the United States was a big move, as you had so many contacts in Mexico. Were you ever apprehensive about the move?*

Maria: Yes, I was a little, as I did not have any friends or relatives here. But I was proud of myself, too, because I was really an adventurer. I chose Los Angeles because I knew that there were a lot of Hispanics there. Unfortunately, I did not know any of them. It turns out that many of the Hispanics there were third-generation

Hispanics who had a big network of friends and family. There were very few first-generation people like myself who were entirely on their own.

Sharon: *Did you have a network of any kind?*

Maria: No, I was on my own and found that the Hispanics living in the United States were very cliquish. They did not share information or embrace newcomers like myself. They did not share their stories, fearing that someone would gain an advantage over them or steal their ideas. It is also important to understand that not all Mexicans living in the United States are from the same socioeconomic strata. Some people, like myself, actually enjoyed a very high standard of living prior to emigrating to the United States. I had servants, a chauffeur, a cook, and other help. In fact, I did not have to bother running my household in Mexico.

Sharon: *I have done some research on immigrant economic adaptation in American. It appears that many women who emigrated here and who had previously enjoyed a high standard of living in their home countries found it difficult to engage in menial chores in the household or in a business setting. Did you also face those kinds of concerns?*

Maria: No. I did not worry about rolling up my shirtsleeves. I was rather looking forward to it. Doing all of these things, in my view, was part of being totally in charge of my own life, which is part of the reason why I chose to emigrate to the United States in the first place and to embrace the American lifestyle.

Sharon: *Looking back, is there anything you would have done differently in planning your move to America? Might it have been smarter, for instance, to have first developed a support network here prior to coming? Or should you have reached out more to your ethnic associations in America?*

Maria: While I definitely think I should have done that, I did not necessarily know how to do so. One always thinks of going to one's embassy or consulate for help, but I have found that that is the last place from which you can get help.

Sharon: *As you were adjusting to America, how was your business faring?*

Maria: By 1983, I had to close down my Mexican travel business. The problem was that the Mexican economy faced a major crisis, and the peso was devalued. My clientele could no longer afford to travel to the United States for their conventions, and the ones who had already booked trips requested refunds. I lost a lot of money in the process, as I had to pay in advance to block the hotels.

Sharon: *What did you do next?*

Maria: At first, I did not know what to do. Obviously the situation was bad in Mexico, so I could not go back there. So, I decided to stay in America and live on my savings until I figured out what to do next. Eventually I had to sell some properties I owned in Mexico to continue to support my family. At this point, however, I had to figure out something else to do. The first thing I thought of was organizing tours from the U.S. to Mexico, but the time was not right: the peso was not established, and the hotels could not provide guarantees. I kept trying, though. I even tried the other way around of bringing goods from Mexico to sell in the United States. This failed because I did not have any connections with distributors, and as a result, I could not gain access to the market.

Finally, my need to get into another business was satisfied when I was led to my current business of making and selling gelatin desserts. This came about because I could not find this dessert in America and I wanted to buy it to serve at home. It is a common dessert in Mexico—the Mexican equivalent of ice cream. It is a snack that we eat in the morning, or at lunch, or during dinnertime. We always served it at birthday parties, along with the birthday cake. I was shocked that it was not available here. As my mother taught me how to prepare this dessert when I was a little girl, I started making it for myself, then for my friends, then for some of my friend's parties, and *viola*—a business idea was born! I decided to call my business LuLu's, as this is my nickname.

Sharon: *How did you plan your new business?*

Maria: First I went to the health department to ascertain their requirements. Next, I began to look for retail space and found a 700 square-foot retail outlet that met the health department's requirements. Then I stocked up my new store: I bought a new sink, a new refrigerator, and all brand new equipment and loads of supplies—and I spent all of my remaining money. I wish I had bought used equipment, but at the time I was so excited I only wanted new things. Unfortunately, however, my excitement did not last long. I was almost out of business in three months! I worked from eight or nine o'clock in the morning to seven or eight o'clock at night, but it was not enough. Furthermore, my gelatin idea was new here and was slow to catch on. I found that I had to add other food like sandwiches, cookies, and other bakery items. But still it did not work out. I realized that in order to increase the sales of my gelatin, I had to locate the first-generation Mexicans who were accustomed to this product. The problem is that I was in the wrong area trying to sell this product. I was not in an area where there were many first-generation Mexicans. But at the time, I did not know where they resided. In fact, where were all the Hispanics were that everyone was talking about I wondered? I didn't even know where to buy Mexican food. So I used to go all the way to the Mexican border to buy Mexican food.

It is really a funny story about how I went about trying to find other first-generation Mexicans living in this country. I got a map and starting driving, but I never really understood how the streets were planned. I found that I did not know where one city began and another one ended. Moreover, I really didn't know how to navigate between north, south, east, and west, because in Mexico, I was not used to navigating with maps. Gradually, I began to realize that my Americanization process entailed more than I knew. I had to learn directions, the culture, the language, and everything, all while suffering from having a lack of friends and family to guide me in the process. There was so much I had to learn. Even navigating the supermarkets was a challenge. One of the things that really impressed me very much when I went to the supermarket is all of the different brands that are available. Take breakfast cereals, for instance. You have more than thirty or forty brands, whereas in Mexico we have six or seven. On balance, I can see that it takes ten years for an immigrant in business to fully understand how to do business in America.

One of the reasons it takes so long to figure America out is that you have such a melting pot of people here with different cultures and different tastes—so really, you have a lot of mini-Americas! I really like it and it is fascinating for me to learn about all of these cultures. But in the beginning it is also very challenging.

Sharon: *Back to the story about your retail outlet selling gelatin products...*

Maria: Let me explain—when I closed my store, I only closed the retail section and converted the space into a small manufacturing plant. I used the space to prepare the product, to package it, and to store it. Once I prepared the gelatin, I put it in the trunk of my car and took it to the areas where the Hispanics stores were in southern California. I heard that the Hispanics were in Wilmington, Carson, Hawthorne, and Inglewood, so I took my products to these areas and found little mom-and-pop stores to which I sold my gelatins on consignment. I told them that there was no obligation on their part, that if they sold it, they could give me the money next week. We entered an agreement on these terms.

Sharon: *Your gelatin was perishable, right? How did you keep it fresh while you traveled around with it?*

Maria: I was only traveling short distances at a time, not far enough for the goods to perish. Now, we have refrigerated trucks that can maintain the freshness of the goods for up to six months at a time.

The good news is that soon my gelatins were selling like hotcakes! My customers were saying *Señora,* please come back. Your gelatins are gone. Everybody loves them. Bring me more tomorrow. My maximum production, at the time, was only 300 cups a day. It was hard to exceed this capacity because the gelatin requires three layers and takes all day to produce. Each layer has to go into the refrigerator to set before the other layer can be added. It wasn't long before I needed more help in the business. I needed more helpers to make it, and I needed distributors to sell it. I also needed to get it onto the shelves of supermarkets. It was clear that I also had to make further investments into the product in order to extend its shelf life so that it could be sold through mass distribution. So, I hired a chemist to help me figure out food preservation strategies. It took me five years to have the formula that I have today! In the meantime, we tried everything, different kinds of preparation processes, different kinds of formulas, et cetera. I remember that I cried many nights before we were able to solve our problem of extending the shelf life of our products.

Sharon: *Were you ever afraid of being sued because of any problems with the gelatin?*

Maria: No, I knew that my products weren't going to make anyone sick. However, I must admit, I was too naïve to know about the problems that could have happened—as they say, ignorance is bliss. If I knew then what I know now I would have never had the nerve to do what I have done, I guarantee you!

So, I merrily went along and continued to grow my business. I moved into a building in Gardenia with 3000 square feet of factory space. I invested a lot to renovate the building to bring it up to the sanitary conditions that were required. Things began to look bright when a new supermarket in the area wanted to carry more Mexican foods. In order to get on the shelves, however, I need to go through a food broker.

Sharon: *What is a food broker?*

Maria: Eighteen years ago, I did not know what one was either until I was called upon by Bill Schwartz of *Concept Food Brokers*. He specifically called on me in response to the request of Mr. Gary Illingworth, a buyer from *The Boys Market*, to get Lulu's product onto the shelves of *The Boys Market*. Bill visited me in my office in Torrance, California and explained the whole food brokerage business. He said that it was typical for food brokers to get 5 percent from the sales of products in return for getting the goods onto store shelves. We made a deal and have worked together for over seventeen years now. When he looks back on our first meeting he laughs about how he had to sit on a milk crate in my office. Anyway, he did indeed help us to get onto the store shelves of some of the smaller stores. And in the meantime, we continued to invest in our food preservation techniques. I went back to Mexico, the heart of the gelatin industry, and hired chemists who knew all about preserving this particular foodstuff. In addition, I also began to educate myself about the process and attended seminars, night classes, and so forth. As I said, altogether it took five years to perfect the process. In the meantime, I began to get more deeply involved with U.S. government regulations and even sought the assistance of the health department to provide advice on preserving my product. However, the main concern of the government was safety in terms of the manufacturing process itself—with which we were in full compliance.

Sharon: *Were you ready break into the global game yet?*

Maria: After penetrating northern and southern California, my next target was the state of Texas. In the meantime, even as my business continued to grow, I continued to handle most functions myself, from invoicing, sales, to marketing. I worked very hard indeed. In fact, I didn't have a sales department until just five years ago, and I have been in business for nineteen years. A major growth spurt occurred in my business when, in 1989, I received a loan backed by the U.S. Small Business Administration (SBA). I was very surprised to be in a partnership with the U.S. government. I wondered why the government would lend me almost a million dollars to expand my business when I didn't even have profit yet.

Sharon: *How do you manage to get the backing of the SBA?*

Maria: I was in the market for a new manufacturing plant. I wanted to have a new space with more refrigeration. Initially, I was looking in L.A. County until a friend of mine told me about a building in Orange County. I went to see it as a courtesy and found that it was a 15,000 square foot abandoned property with over 8000 square feet of refrigeration. While no one else was in the market for this, it was a blessing for me. The building cost $1.2 million. Although this was a lot of money and more than I planned to spend, I decided to go for it and made an offer to the owner. The owner did not respond. However, because I was a woman and an Hispanic, he couldn't believe that I was going to be able get a loan. My broker stepped in on my behalf and assured that owner that I was pre-approved for my loan. My loan had the backing of SBA's guarantee, which was an arrangement organized by the bank itself. Nevertheless, I felt that there was some discrimination involved, and it was the first time I ever experienced it in America. In the end, I was able to acquire the property and came to an understanding with the seller, who later even gave me a second note on the property.

I didn't meet the owner until six years later, when I went to meet him in order to pay off my debt in person. I particularly wanted to do this in person, because, unfortunately, things took a turn for the worse during the period of 1991 to 1994. At that time I could only pay the interest on the second note. I was glad to finally meet him in person, as we Latinos are accustomed to doing business in person. You don't just mail a check and leave it at that. When I finally met him, I showed him photos of my manufacturing plant and I thanked him for his patience and paid him the balance that I owed him. I told him that in the future he should believe in women in business, especially Latinas, because we live up to our obligations and commitments.

Sharon: *Please explain how and when you began to export.*

Maria: I became involved with exporting in a major way through a new company that I started in 1990 with a new partner, an industrial engineer who was working for a "fruit bar" company. Because I had extra space in my building, we decided he could use share the space with LuLu's. We formed a company called "Fancy Fruit" and became 50/50 partners, although I put up all the money. As my partner claimed to have had a lot of exporting experience, I relied upon him to chart our new export course to sell "Fancy Fruit" frozen fruit bars and LuLu's gelatin desserts at the same time.

As it turns out, he did not know as much about exporting as he claimed. Consequently, I lost a lot of money, and our exporting ventures failed. Over the course of our partnership I began to spend money at a rate faster than I was taking it in, as I was not yet operating to full capacity in my facility. Soon I found that I had to sell some more property to keep my head above water. Then the recession hit, and my mortgages were higher than the value of the real estate I was holding. I almost went bankrupt and had to send all of my belongings back to Mexico. I also had to return one of my properties to that bank that I couldn't sell. In addition, I lost one of my manufacturing plants and one of my income properties. At the same time, in 1992, my father passed away. I was already very depressed when the IRS came after me for some payroll taxes I owed. I kept slipping further behind and was in bad shape. It took me five years to get out of this trouble. I am glad to say that I eventually paid everything off, but it was a very expensive lesson.

Sharon: *Summarize why you think your export business failed.*

Maria: Our export business failed for two main reasons. First, we did not engage in the proper planning, and secondly, we did not know enough about export financing. In particular, we did not operate on the basis on confirmed Letters of Credit (L/Cs); instead, we shipped on open account and were screwed out of our money on a number of occasions. I don't think my negative experiences in exporting were unique, especially for small new-to-exporting firms.

Let me give you some examples of some of the mistakes we made in exporting. One customer from England called and said that he wanted to import our fruit bars. He flew over to meet us, and we struck a deal. He gave us a small deposit and we sent him his full order. It then took him six months to pay us. A similar scenario ensued with regard to a major shipment to Chile. This buyer purchased our fruit bars and paid for his first order in full. Subsequently, he gave us a series of checks in Chilean pesos that were to be deposited at later dates. We deposited the checks and they bounced! Our losses didn't end there, however. We had to hire a lawyer in Chile to try to collect the money, but it was never collected. In another example, one of my partner's friends from New Zealand placed a large order with us. There were six or seven large shipments involved. He paid us for the first three and then failed to pay for the last three shipments, which were worth $150,000. We never got this money back.

Sharon: *As you had already been involved with SBA, and as they have an international department that provides export working capital guarantees, did you ever consider approaching them to learn how to get their guarantees to cover your export shipments?*

Maria: No, I did not. To be honest with you, Sharon, I never knew about their international products and services until two years ago. My involvement with SBA was limited to my domestic operations. It is only recently that I have taken the time to fully investigate the resources of various government agencies like the SBA. Now that I am out in the world, talking with people and researching the different government agencies, I understand better how to do business, how to export, and how to call upon the resources of the government when needed. I don't feel ashamed to tell you this because this happened to me, and I know there are thousands of people like me who go into exporting without fully preparing themselves to do so.

Sharon: *The findings from a survey of women exporters that I undertook for the SBA in conjunction with a recent Canada-U.S. Business Women's Summit showed that many women are shipping on open account—which essentially means that they are trusting their buyers to pay. If their buyers do not pay under such circumstances, they have no recourse. So, what did you do with your partner in the end?*

Maria: I am happy to tell you that I finally bought out my partner in November 1999, but it was very costly. I had to pay him 50 percent of the value of the firm, settle all of the bad debts, and write off the loans I made to the company. Although we lost a lot of money in exporting, it did not sour me on the potential of exporting. I now know that we have to do it in a smarter way. In the first year alone, under the guidance of my partner, we lost almost a $1 million in our export business.

I have since had a chance to fully analyze where and how we lost money in exporting. Some of it was due to nonpayment, but we also lost in other ways. For instance, we lost money because of our wrapping and packaging strategies. We lost money on our labeling strategies and approaches—for instance, we printed names of distributors in different countries who subsequently went out of business, et cetera.

Sharon: *Do you think that you would have made these mistakes without your partner?*

Maria: If I were doing it entirely on my own, I would have undertaken more research and engaged in more planning. As a consequence, perhaps I would have done things differently. As it was, however, I had full faith and confidence in my partner, especially at the beginning. When things started to go wrong, he continued to represent that he knew what he was doing and that things would turn around. When you are very busy, as I was, I felt that it was important to rely on my partner's advice.

Sharon: *What impact did your export experience have on your overall business?*

Maria: Fancy Fruit stunted the growth of LuLu's desserts from its inception. Not only did we lose a lot of money through our failed export operations that constrained overall growth, but in addition, the operations of Fancy Fruit took up half of the operating space within our combined manufacturing facility. Because we lacked space for LuLu's gelatin desserts, I had to lease another building, which was not only costly, but it also constrained our ability to develop new products.

            Over the period of four years I investigated the possibility of building a new food processing plant for LuLu's in South Orange County. At one point, I had gone so far as to map out all of the planning details. At the last moment I decided not to buy it because I did not feel confident that I would be able to find laborers who would be willing to work for $6 or $7 an hour, given the strength of the economy. I decided to contact the State of California to figure out how they could help me and to get their advice on whether I should build this plant or not.

Sharon: *It sounds like this is the first time that you ever really pulled yourself back before going ahead.*

Maria: Yes, that is right. For the first time, based in part on the advice of others, I stopped and carefully weighed all options. In the meantime, I was introduced to a new property in Vernon (Los Angeles). The 65,000 square foot property, which includes a processing plant, is in an industrial area and used to belong to Baskin and Robbins. I negotiated over a five-month period with the Real Estate Department of Allied Domecq in Massachusetts, which owns Baskin and Robbins, to purchase the property. The plant is perfect for LuLu's because it has all of the necessary food processing facilities and equipment that will enable LuLu's Desserts to accelerate the pace of its growth and to make up for lost time. I feel really blessed that after all of my travails, I have been able to acquire a facility of the standard of Baskin and Robbins. Can you imagine how I feel? I am a woman, a Latina, and an immigrant, who despite having many challenges has been able to step up to the plate and negotiate with the world's second largest international spirits and food service group. Wow! I cannot even mention this back in Mexico because no one there could possibly believe it. You can only do this in America! This plant in Vernon will be our second LuLu's plant; our plant in Huntington Beach will be the headquarters for LuLu's Dessert and will also produce for our Fancy Fruit operation. It is thrilling, and I am so excited!

I must say that I love the thrill of the deal. So of course, I am into some other deals. Right now, I have a 70,000 square foot property on 3.6 acres that I want to develop. I am looking for just the right client—do you know any, Sharon?

Sharon: *Maria, you are the hot property. Everyone must be courting you. Have state governments been offering you incentives to do business in their states?*

Maria: Interestingly, when the State of California heard that I was considering the property in Vernon, they convened their "Red Team," which includes the Edison Company, to figure out how to provide me with attractive incentives to do the deal. They wanted to keep the 110 jobs my company created in the area. The Edison Company offered me credit of $110,000 to pay for my electricity, and the state offered free employee training. I was so moved. For the first time in all of these years, I finally felt like I was not alone.

A small bidding war ensued to capture my business. The State of Illinois tried to attract me to come to Chicago, and then Hamlin, in the State of Texas, tried to do the same. Now I see a big potential and the different opportunities from which I can choose. After all the attention, I can tell you that as of forty-eight hours ago,

I made my decision and should have the new building as of October 2000. I am happy now that my employees will have better working conditions and that we will have room in which to grow.

Sharon: *It is an appropriate time to ask you how you measure your success and how your measures have changed over the years.*

Maria: Honestly, in the beginning when I was very small, I didn't have any idea of how big I could become. Frankly, I didn't even know whether I could survive. Then little by little I got excited about the opportunities in this country. Only here could I have accomplished what I did. What enables small business growth in this country is the developed network of businesses and infrastructure to support business. In addition, there is a high degree of specialization throughout the chain; the manufacturers know their business, as do the distributors, the retailers, and all of the others in the chain from the shop to the consumer. By contrast, in Mexico, various parts of the business support system don't function properly. I opened a distribution company in Mexico in 1992, but I had to close my doors in Mexico after two years due to the devaluation of the peso. Before I closed, however, I got a firsthand look into some of the problems of operating there. There are many constraints to doing business there. I wish that I could help, but I fear that it will take many years to change.

My mission now is to expand my company and to educate consumers about my gelatin product. When I first got into this business no one understood the word *gelatin*. They only knew about Jell-O. And the funny thing is, I can't even pronounce that word. Our product is not Jell-O; it is a healthy gelatin dessert product with fruit in between the layers. We have a variety of fifty products in gelatin alone, and twenty-five different flavors of frozen fruit bars. Next year, we are launching a new chocolate-dipped fruit bar, in five different fruit flavors.

Our new challenge is to find ways of entering new domestic and foreign markets. On the domestic front, one of our goals is to penetrate school systems, food service consortia, and major conglomerates like McDonalds. Incidentally, we are currently in the process of being approved by McDonalds to be included in their food group. On the international front, we want to start manufacturing our product in foreign countries. We are also enthusiastic about the prospect of expanding our exports into new markets, and we are increasingly utilizing the resources of government agencies to help us in this endeavor. The difficulty is managing the dynamism in our company.

Sharon: *Why are you so keen on exporting?*

Maria: It's embarrassing to say, but I have tried to penetrate the frozen food sections of major supermarkets for the past 10 years to no avail. Large companies like Haagen Das, Unilever, Carnation, and others more or less monopolize these sections. They pay what is called a "slotting allowance" to the supermarkets, and that's how they get this space in the frozen food section of the stores. If you are too small to pay these entry costs, then you don't have a chance of getting onto the shelves. So far, I have spent a lot of money in trying to get into the frozen food sections, but so far to no avail. The cycle starts every summer of trying to get in, but no matter how hard we have tried, we have not yet been successful. So, for my business, in some respects, it is easier to break into export markets than it is to break into the U.S. mainstream—which is sad to say but true. I believe that foreign markets will appreciate the quality of our products, the beauty of our packaging, our exotic fruits, and will more readily allow us to break into their frozen food sections.

Sharon: *As you further reflect upon your export experience, what advice would you give readers about how to export?*

Maria: First, I would advise them to develop a comprehensive business plan for the period of five to ten years. I underscore the need to plan for the future. I know as a Latin immigrant that we were not educated to plan for the long term, just as we are not trained to use maps to chart our geographic directions. We are used to stumbling around in the dark, feeling our way through. This is partially because we, as Latinos, are not accustomed to sharing ideas, believing that someone will steal them from us. It does not have to be like that, though. We can shed light on each other's path.

Secondly, I also advise women to endeavor to integrate new technologies into their plans. E-commerce, for instance, makes exporting so much easier than in the past. We have to stay current and not stick to doing things the way we did in the past. We also have to get involved in organizations that help us to stay current and abreast of the latest information.

Finally, we should never be too busy to fully investigate what we are doing. Just think of the money I could have saved had I taken the time to learn about the export guarantees of EXIM Bank. Instead, I relied on my partner, and he didn't know any more than I did. In retrospect, I should have called upon the resources of trade associations and government officials to help me properly plan my export business. These agencies have a lot of information to help exporters. They even have offices overseas that have counselors who can provide expert advice on how to do business in the country. In addition, these offices of the U.S. Department of Commerce and located in the U.S. embassies abroad can also provide lists of importers and exporters, agents, and distributors. If I knew then what I know now about the assistance available for exporters, I would have shut my partner down a long time ago and could have had sources of checks and balances against what he was telling me.

Sharon: *And what about export financing? What lessons have you learned that you would like to share?*

Maria: I know about working capital guarantees and about export insurance and now, I don't make an export move without these assurances. I just signed an agreement for export insurance last month, and now I feel safe and secure in my export operations. I am also exploring opportunities with the Overseas Private Investment Corporation (OPIC), which provides insurance for investments overseas and some grant funds to study proposed investments. The only reason I didn't do this before is because I did not know that it was possible to do it. I simply did not have the information. My constraint at present is that I need to have an export planning department to focus on this aspect of our business. At present, I am using student interns, but I need to have a budget to hire someone full time.

Sharon: *What lessons have you learned about management that you would like to share?*

Maria: I have grown to the point that I have finally formalized all of the departments within my company. Each department, including our newly established human resources department, now operates professionally and with responsibility. I had to grow into this, however. Now that I am at this point, we can operate more efficiently and effectively as an organization. I am currently reinvesting all of my profits into the company. In a few years, who knows? I may consider going public, or a merging with another operation. I have to confess, though, that our fast growth scares me a little.

Sharon: *What about growing faster and bigger scares you?*

Maria: Because there are no limits, I really can't predict where I'll be or what I'll be doing in a few years. It is an unpredictable life in a way, but it is exciting, and I learn constantly. The scary part is that I have won so many awards recently that I feel obliged to continue. Otherwise, I'll let everyone down, especially my Latina sisters. I never had this pressure before when I was anonymous.

Sharon: *This is the first time I heard you mention the word* fear. *Do you have any fears?*

Maria: Yes, in fact, I have many fears, especially of the unknown. It is just that I am not consumed or destroyed by my fears. I still live every day of my life very intensely. I try to remember that no matter what happens, I give thanks to God for allowing me to have this opportunity in my life. I am very happy and very proud of who I am and of what I have accomplished. No one can ever take that away from me. I don't regret my decision to leave my family and my country 20 years ago. Yes, I had to suffer a lot, but in the end, I benefited enormously and it was the best decision I ever made in my life. I have been able to visit the world and grow in my outlook and in my business. My life in Mexico, by contrast, was very limited.

I also find strength in knowing that no matter what happens, I can always start over. I know that I have the strength to fight the battles I must fight. Indeed, I have been a good warrior when I had to be, like when I had to fight my ex-husband, who took my eldest daughter Maria de Lourdes back to Mexico when she was twelve years old. She is now twenty-four years and I have not seen her since she was taken back to Mexico.

I have also had to prove myself in battle against my ex-partner, who tried to take over Fancy Fruit. I won that battle, fortunately.

Despite my various troubles, I am strengthened by the realization that although nineteen years ago everybody was laughing at my ideas and thought I was crazy, I have proven them wrong. My own family was not sure about my decision to move to the United States alone and to start my own business. I am, after all, the only one from my family who looked for new horizons and the only adventurer among my five siblings—the others are all attorneys. I am the only one in business. It was hard for them to understand my newly acquired American mentality that places such a high premium on hard work. They would see me working so hard and ask, Why? I tell them I have started something that I cannot stop. I have an enormous responsibility to my employees, my customers, my supplies, my brokers, and to many others—I cannot let them down.

My kind of business, manufacturing, is male dominated in my home country. It often requires one to roll up one's sleeves and to get dirty. My own family felt sorry for me to have to stoop to this level. However, they now understand that my work is honorable, that it is a privilege, and that I am worthy of and have earned their respect for having thrived and succeeded in such a difficult endeavor.

My father passed away in 1992. He had been one of the greatest civil attorneys in Mexico. He expected me to become an attorney, too, but I chose a business career instead. He was upset with me for many years and considered me to be a rebellious daughter. It took my father ten years to accept me as a businesswoman in America. When he visited my new plant and saw the full fruit bar operation in action, he finally realized that I was seriously in business, that I was in it for the long haul, and that I was not going to give up. I earned my father's acceptance and my mother's love and support, and also that of the world. Most importantly, however, I am proud of myself and the vision I had to turn my mother's family gelatin recipe into the basis of a growing manufacturing business that is making new inroads into the food industry in America and in the world. The amazing coincidence is that when I dreamed of coming to America, I never dreamt of coming here to commercialize a traditional Mexican dessert recipe. But I am happy that it worked out that way, as I have combined a bit of the old world with the new world.

I want to take this opportunity before closing to thank all of the people who believed in me, including my daughter Monica, who is thirteen years old, and who I hope takes over this business one day. And without the support of my family, friends, and loyal staff I would not be able to continue my journey in making my American and global dreams come true.

And to the readers, I want to say that although we may come from different ethnic backgrounds, we are similar in pursuing our entrepreneurial endeavors and similarly, we must also accept a responsibility to make the world a better place in which to live as we pursue our dreams.

I am looking forward to conquering new global frontiers with a little help from the sugar, water, fruit, and passion that come together to form LuLu's Dessert.

* * *

Candace Chen
President
PowerClean 2000

Contact:

PowerClean 2000

3710 Avalon Blvd.
Los Angeles, CA 90011-5660

Phone: (323) 235-2000
Fax: (323) 235-6259
Email: candace@powerclean2000.com
Web: http://www.powerclean2000.com

LORI SHEPLER / Los Angeles Times

Candace Chen displays some of Power Clean 2000's machines in the company's South-Central Los Angeles factory.

Risky Business

Exporters Find That the China Trade Can Be Treacherous

By DON LEE, TIMES STAFF WRITER

ENTERPRISE ZONE
*Lessons and Insight on
Southland Businesses*

Like many U.S. exporters, Candace Chen believes that no country holds as much potential as China. But after six long years of contending with bureaucrats, counterfeiters and kidnappers, the 28-year-old president of **Power Clean 2000** Inc. is understandably weary.

Since late 1991, Chen's South-Central Los Angeles business, which makes machines and solvents that remove carbon from car engines, has plowed more than $2 million into China. Power Clean had two good years there, but then knockoffs wiped out the company's sales and, in one instance, blew up a car, for which Power Clean got blamed. It only got worse in 1996, when a band of thugs in Shanghai abducted Chen's father, demanding that he sign a ransom note and that Power Clean get out of the country.

Chen, a diminutive but tough woman known as the "queen of decarbonization" in China, has not given up. Determined to make a profit in China, the Taiwanese-born lawyer and keeper of her small family business has filed lawsuits abroad and complained vigorously to senior trade officials in Beijing and Washington. "I'm still optimistic," she says.

Lured by China's vast potential market, a growing number of small businesses in the Southland have ventured to the country in recent years. Some have succeeded, thanks partly to contacts made through the U.S. Department of Commerce. And now more businesses are turning to China in hopes that it could help offset plunging sales in other Asian countries wallowing in financial crisis.

China, with plenty of foreign reserves, relatively little short-term debt and a market and currency less accessible to outsiders, has not caught the current Asian economic contagion.

The latest trade data is also promising. California's exports to China jumped 39% in 1998 to almost $2 billion, and they were up 11% in the first half of last year, even as exports to Japan, South Korea, Singapore and Malaysia slipped badly and the state's total exports grew by just 2% in the first half of 1997. As

Please see ENTERPRISE, D6

Candace Chen
President and CEO, PowerClean 2000

Sharon: *Candace, having served with you now for two years on the U.S. Commerce Department's and the U.S. Trade Representative's Industry Sector Advisory Committee on Small and Minority Business (ISAC 14), I have observed that you are a very regal person but even I did not know that you were a Queen until I read the article in the Los Angeles Times and learned that you are known as the "Queen of Decarbonization." I certainly knew that you were special however and that you know an awful lot about doing business overseas. Through your business advocacy work, including your senior position on the Trans Atlantic Business Council, and through your exporting business, you are considered by many to be one of our nation's leading experts on trade. I am very happy therefore that you have agreed to tell us your story firsthand so that we can learn from your vast international business experience. How did you get started?*

Candace: I was in law school and just turned twenty-two years old when I went into business. My brother had invented a process by which carbon deposits inside gasoline and diesel engines could be economically removed in less than an hour, without having to take the engine apart. The benefits of this process were performance-related; it increased fuel economy, enhanced horsepower, prolonged engine life, and led to significant reductions in particulate emissions.

As I was so young when I started out, going into business was probably more of a life decision than a business decision per se. I was grateful to my brother for entrusting this invention to me. I had a choice between pursuing a career as a real estate lawyer once I graduated from law school, or taking on the challenge of promoting a product that had potential for exponential growth. I chose the latter, believing that I could be a lawyer anytime but that the opportunity to market this product would only be once in a lifetime. My brother is a quiet intellectual, whereas I have been the obnoxious, pushy little sister who has always taken the reins of control ever since I was a little girl. Even though I was only twenty-two when I went into business, I had prior business-related experience, having worked in wholesale merchandising on a part-time basis as a teenager. I had also obtained my real estate agent's license when I was just eighteen years old and had sold real estate part-time to support my college and law school education. In short, I felt comfortable to take on this business venture.

Sharon: *As you have always been a take-charge person, to what extent did wanting to be your own boss influence your decision to start a business?*

Candace: Being fresh out of college, it wasn't so much the desire to be my own boss as much as the challenge and practicality of marketing the product line. The product concept was innovative back in 1991, as it remains today. Starting a company to support the product line seemed like the logical thing to do, but it certainly is not for the faint-hearted. Some of my friends, as well as young women that I meet in social settings, often tell me how much they envy my independence. Some find the public policy forums and the networking I am involved in to be glamorous, and they have sought my advice about quitting their jobs to start a business. My advice is always the same: It is not a decision to take lightly! In addition to the heavy financial investments, much blood, sweat, and tears goes into starting a business from scratch and maintaining it. Being the boss also can mean being awake at night worrying about the source of the next payroll. In my case, being in the automotive industry literally meant rolling up my sleeves and getting greasy elbows when called upon to demonstrate our products.

It is funny that, in some regards, the tables have turned. While many women are figuring out how to be their own boss, some men are figuring out how not to be the boss. Case in point: several years ago, I was traveling with a very competent and at the time unemployed associate whom I had known for some time. Unbeknownst to him, I had considered offering him a senior position at the company. Our conversation turned to the subject of managerial expertise, and he said with conviction that anyone who aspired to be the head of any business venture is an idiot. I was curious and asked him to explain. He said that as senior management he would have the power to do practically as he pleases and would have only his boss to fear. However, if his decisions became detrimental for the company and the sky began falling, then the sky would fall upon the boss's head before it hit his. That was the last time I spoke with the man.

Sharon: *How have you handled issues of control and delegation in your business?*

Candace: You may have guessed that I am somewhat of a control freak. I like to be informed of the progress of our projects and also have a tendency to want to take over the project if I feel that the person to whom I have assigned it has not followed my instructions. Needless to say, that has resulted in some hard feelings for those involved and exhausts me physically. It took a while, but I finally came to realize the value of teamwork and the fact that I cannot give all my projects sufficient attention when I force myself to take on more than I can realistically handle. I used to joke that I run my company like an army, with strict rules and discipline. But now I am more relaxed and lenient. We have also changed the basic operating philosophy of our firm, from having a sizable in-house assembly force to one that utilizes outside contractors in order to cut down on overhead. We are not manufacturers per se, as we do not make our metal cabinets or parts from raw materials. We are more like an assembly house, sourcing and coordinating parts from different vendors and then putting them together to make the final product. We believe that it is important to have a good working relationship with our suppliers. Although we could easily work only with the largest vendors of our required products, we find that sometimes the small companies are more flexible and offer more personalized service.

Sharon: *How did you measure success when you started your business?*

Candace: Manufacturing is a very traditional business. As a manufacturer of automotive service products, we measured success in very tangible and traditional terms, such as in terms of how well we were doing financially and our position in the industry. However, because our products are technology based, we invested heavily in research and development to make sure that we were always ahead of the competition.

Sharon: *Why did you want to go global, and when did you do it?*

Candace: We began exporting for several reasons and took our first step in 1992. We knew that the product had global appeal, regardless of the economy of the markets. Wherever there were gasoline and diesel engines, whether in use in cars, boats, buses, generators, cranes, or in trains, there would be a need to economically optimize the performance of the engines involved in order to reduce the cost of operation and to benefit the environment.

As with any new technology in the automotive industry, automaker endorsement is crucial to popularize the product. However, soon after we began calling on the Big Three (GM, Ford, Chrysler), it became apparent that product merit was not the first thing they considered when new technology was involved. Because we were a small firm without the requisite contacts in Detroit, no one would take our calls, let alone endorse our technology. As a result, we switched our marketing focus from domestic to foreign markets, as we believed the latter would be more receptive to innovative U.S. technology. Thus, we decided to penetrate the global market, gain a position, and then come back and focus on the domestic market.

Sharon: *Going global was very important to your business growth strategy then?*

Candace: Indeed, we gained invaluable experience from working with a vast array of engines in very disparate terrains and weather conditions. As a result, we were able to improve and enhance our technology. Now we are far ahead of our competition.

Sharon: *How have you changed the way you measure your firm's success, and what impact has globalization had on your firm's success?*

Candace: We have definitely developed a more philosophical, global, and quality-oriented outlook. Meeting the challenges we faced overseas underscored the importance of developing appropriate solutions for different problems. I am glad to say that we developed this experience base early on in our business. We can honestly say, therefore, that even though making money is important, maintaining a reputation of high performance standards is money in the bank. We have all heard of the saying that diamonds are a girl's best friend. In our opinion, *solid reputation is a small firm's best friend.*

Sharon: *What are some of the challenges your firm has faced in going global?*

Candace: Clearly, there are times in the course of business when the choice between opting for instant financial gratification versus upholding the highest quality standards is posed. Such choices may be presented in many forms, some more subtle than others. For instance, one situation with which we are frequently faced is the matter of exclusivity of representation. Many foreign firms will insist upon an exclusive agreement with the U.S. manufacturer because of the magnitude of the investment involved in the marketing and distribution of a new product line. However, very often a local customer or competitor of the distributor will contact the factory directly with an offer to purchase a substantial amount of product without the knowledge of the factory's official country distributor. In such cases we are faced with a dilemma. Do we opt for the instant financial gratification, or do we uphold our integrity, our corporate standards, and our loyalty to our partners? Although such offers are tempting, we have always directed these inquiries back to our distributor. We assure the would-be buyers that if they have a genuine interest in our products, it is our official distributor who would be in the best position to offer timely and personal service. Unfortunately, we have heard of many American companies that do not uphold their promises to their foreign partners. We believe that this is a mistake and very short sighted. In our case, in a specialty niche product business, word of such unsavory business practices would travel very fast and ultimately undermine our long-term position. Because we have developed and maintained a solid and reliable reputation, not only have we earned the loyalty of foreign partners, we have also increasingly been sought out by prominent domestic clients who entrust us with custom and private label projects.

Sharon: *Clearly, being able to make tough choices is an important part of what you had to learn. What are some of the other lessons you had to learn in doing your global business?*

Candace: As our export activities steadily increased over the years, we began to realize that going global was more complicated than just finding buyers and getting paid. There were a number of external issues, from differing technical standards to unfair tariffs and intellectual property rights infringements that profoundly affected our business. We also found that we were not the only firm whose activities were affected by these barriers. In fact, such trade barriers are common to many SMEs (small medium size enterprises). We have realized, however, that the U.S. government offers many effective channels through which we can address such issues and seek protection and redress. Therefore, during the last several years, we have taken part in trade policy forums to help our government representatives understand the practical, real world aspects of trade barriers that affect small companies on a daily basis.

Sharon: *How did you prepare to go global initially?*

Candace: The possibility of exporting was one that was always on my mind, even before we opened our doors. There was no doubt in my mind that we would eventually reach out to the global market: I knew that there would be tremendous demand in foreign markets for products that reduced vehicle emissions and cut operation costs. However, because the costs involved in attending foreign trade shows were prohibitively high, we started by showing our products at major domestic industry shows in the hope of attracting foreign buyers. We sold some product and made some connections, but it clearly was not enough to sustain the momentum and enter new markets. Luckily, during one of the shows we attended, a U.S. Department of Commerce (DOC) trade specialist came by our booth and introduced us to the programs that DOC offered to help companies export. I was skeptical at the time and questioned the person's motive. It should be underscored that I had no previous experience dealing with government agencies; for me there was no difference between the U.S. Department of Commerce and the Internal Revenue Service. I learned, however, that the U.S.

government had a lot to offer and, in the end, was very instrumental in helping to launch our export activities.

Sharon: *How long did it take you to plan your business before you started it?*

Candace: It took approximately one year to research various markets in terms of supply-and-demand considerations. We also had to analyze the financing considerations pursuant to market entry and market penetration. Once the decision was made to start the business, finding suitable manufacturing facilities, office space, and recruiting personnel all came together relatively quickly. In the course of the preparation, I specifically remembered one scenario—shopping for office furniture. Being a new business with limited resources, I decided to look through classified ads for used furniture. The man who ultimately sold us his lot of office equipment and furniture had just closed his business and moved everything into his garage. As I went to pick up the furniture from the seller's garage, he had a strange look on his face when I picked up the lot with a borrowed truck. I could not tell whether he was happy to have his garage emptied, or relieved to be rid of the remnants of his failed business. I could not help but sympathize with him, but at the same time I also promised myself that I would not suffer the same fate.

Upon reflection, I can say that engaging in adequate preparation is crucial to the success of any new business. One should have a detailed business plan and take the time to research its feasibility and to learn as much about the industry as possible. Even more time should be spent in this process in cases where entrepreneurs, like me, are new to the industry.

Having said this, it is very difficult to plan for the unexpected. In the beginning, practically every day was an adventure and a proving ground for trials and errors. However, having an open mind and flexibility in business dealings are as important as preparing for the unexpected.

Sharon: *What were the key factors you took into consideration in planning your global business?*

Candace: On the top of our list were such considerations as whether there was a demand for the product in given countries, and if not, whether it could be created. We also scrutinized foreign government regulations with respect to vehicle emissions and ascertained whether distribution channels existed. Other important considerations included whether we could find suitable partners, whether there was local competition, and most importantly, we assessed the risk of patent and copyright infringements.

In addition to the foregoing, we spent time studying the culture and social customs of various countries in which we had an interest. This helped us tailor our program toward local consumer mentality and helped to ensure that we would not inadvertently offend our potential clients. While all of the considerations are important, I believe the universal factor for success in doing business globally in the long run is to establish the ability to support the customer. Therefore, anyone looking to expand their business overseas should realistically evaluate their ability to support the product once it is exported. Choosing the right agent, distributors, and technical representative partners overseas is key to having the ability to support the product on the ground. Therefore, special care should be given in choosing the right partners.

Sharon: *What were your biggest fears about going global?*

Candace: I don't think that I have ever been afraid of going global. There have been plenty of bumps in the road, from local competitors who infringe upon our patent by copying our products, to clients' misuse of our products, but nothing that we have come across is really unusual in the normal course of business. However, in our particular situation, the biggest bump in the road is the need to educate our customers about the product. Educating our potential partners about the need and strategy for the product, followed by the more difficult task of educating the public about the benefits to the environment and their pocket books, is our major strategic challenge.

On the personal front, being a youthful looking woman in a traditionally male industry might have been a cause for initial concern about whether I would be accepted. In fact, this has turned out to be the source of many amusing incidents. Several years ago, for instance, I had corresponded with a perspective Asian client. One day, the gentleman called my office and, much to his surprise, discovered that I was a woman. Nevertheless, as he was coming to Los Angeles, he wanted to visit our facility. I made an arrangement to meet him at the lobby of a luxury downtown hotel. When I waited in the hotel lobby, I noticed an older Asian gentleman taking a walk in the lobby area. However, every time he approached me, he would look away and go right pass me. Finally, on his fourth or fifth trip, I decided to ask him if he was my visitor, and he said he was. He apologized for his unusual behavior and explained that even though he knew I was a woman, he assumed that I would be older, if not elderly!

Sharon: *A funny incident like that just happened to me as well. I was headhunted for an important short-term assignment in Bosnia. The search team had put many candidates before the boss, who was an elderly American Jewish man who was representing the U.S. government in the position to which I would report. He refused all possible candidates until he came to my resume; he liked it and chose me sight unseen. He traveled to the United States to meet with me before I took up the post. In the hotel lobby where we arranged to meet, I was the only female and certainly the only one wearing what I had informed him I'd be wearing. However, because my name is Sharon Freeman, he thought I was Jewish and could not put my African American face and appearance together with the resume he knew so well.*

Back to your story: Who provided advice to you on planning your global business?

Candace: Being partners in business, my brother and I have always discussed our business strategies and decisions before we implemented them. Some of the seminars and workshops offered by the U.S. Department of Commerce through its network of U.S. Export Assistance Centers (USEACs) have been especially helpful. These workshops range from basic export marketing and documentation, to product certification and financing. I tend to gravitate toward those that are lead by fellow business owners who have personally experienced the trials and tribulations of running a small business, rather than by academics, who although informative are confined to the theoretical. Global strategies and export assistance programs offered by the local export assistance centers are also useful and tend to be more economical than those offered by universities and professional organizations.

Sharon: *What sources of information have you used to find relevant global information?*

Candace: Before the Internet became a popular and affordable tool, I did much of my research in the local library and ordered sector-specific information through industry associations. I found another good source of information when I began working with a trade specialist at the local export assistance center. I found that the U.S. government, through its network of offices domestically and overseas, as well as sector-specific units in Washington, has a wealth of information that is both updated and either free or very affordable. I have seen much of the same information compiled by professional marketing firms and resold to the public for hundreds and sometimes thousand of dollars.

Sharon: *How do you develop and draw on contacts?*

Candace: Most of my contacts are developed through either product promotion activities, such as trade shows, or general business networking. Although a major industry trade show with international attendance is the natural venue for developing potential clients, these shows have not been useful for our company. We found that the majority of foreign visitors at these shows did not understand English well enough to be able to grasp the concept of our product. Trade shows are probably helpful for companies that sell conventional off-the-shelf items, but for technological innovations that require concept explanation, the language barrier under trade show conditions was difficult to resolve. We have found that it is important for our potential clients to have ample time to digest the product concept and research its potential. We also make sure that they ask as many questions as are necessary to not only to put them at ease, but also for us to gauge their interest in representing our firm.

During the course of running our business, I have become a member in several local trade associations. While the networking events have a great deal of potential to help service firms identify new clientele, in our case, they have not been helpful. To the contrary, general service contractors who want to sell our firm their services often bombard me. The actual buyers for our type of products seldom attended these events. We stopped going to these events, but we stay active in ones that have an international or sector specific theme.

Because of my Asian heritage and appearance, most people like to ask where I am from. I always tell them I am from Los Angeles to establish the fact that I am an American, and then I appease their curiosity by telling them about my Taiwanese/Chinese heritage. In doing business internationally, I find that it is necessary not only to establish credibility for the firm and products, but for me as president of the company, especially given my youthful appearance. Most foreign partners appreciate information about my educational background and professional accomplishments.

I have also learned through observing other women that many of us have a tendency to mishandle well-deserved compliments. A common example is when a female executive is complimented for her performance in a public forum. Rather than a mere thank you, some would couple that with a statement about how nervous or asinine she thought she was. Personally, I don't think that responding to a compliment by demeaning oneself demonstrates modesty; rather, it implies that the other person was an idiot for not having seen how you really presented yourself. I also noticed that in comparison to men, women have a tendency to apologize when the occasion does not call for an apology. When expected at a meeting, I do not like to apologize for being late, if I was not at fault. Instead, I thank those who arrived before I did for their patience and follow with a one-sentence explanation for the delay, and promptly proceed with the meeting.

Sharon: *What kinds of networks have been the most beneficial in building your global business?*

Candace: There are basically three types of networks that are beneficial for our business: industry-specific networks, government-related networks, and general business networks. While developing and maintaining our industry-specific contacts is our most important task, broadening our network to include contacts throughout the United States and among foreign governments is also important, as is developing and maintaining our network of service companies, bankers, freight forwarders, accountants, and lawyers.

Networking can be a challenge, however. Even though I have an outgoing personality and seem at ease at any networking event, I was not always like this. In fact, shortly after I passed my California real estate agent's exam, one of the major real estate franchises in my home area invited me to their annual Christmas party. It was very intimidating. There were about 300 to 500 people present. The room was lavishly decorated with abundant seafood platters, huge expensive exotic centerpieces, and champagne flowing from sculptured ice blocks. I remember going in, surveying the room, bumping into crowds around me, and smiling at everyone who met my eyes. Yet, the truth is that I was so uncomfortable. I quickly made my way through the crowd and went home without speaking to anyone. It was a good lesson for me. On my way home, I thought about my behavior and knew that if I was going to succeed in life, I must force myself to change. I later began to seek out opportunities to attend social events, starting with small ones where I knew at least several people, and then graduating to larger holiday events where I hardly knew anyone. Today, I am happy to say that there are very few events, if any, at which I would feel uncomfortable. I am now fully capable of working any room.

Sharon: *What strategies have you employed to build your contacts overseas?*

Candace: As a manufacturer, our primary foreign contacts are clients who represent our product line or agents who work with us to find suitable partners. Some of these contacts find us through trade advertisements, while we meet others through U.S. Department of Commerce-sponsored trade missions or networking sessions that have an international theme.

Sharon: *How important are contacts overseas for being successful globally?*

Candace: Contacts overseas are very important. The most important contacts for our firm are our current or potential clients. In order to identify new clients, however, we rely on a network of local business acquaintances and on the U.S. embassy and consulate in the target foreign country. We particularly value the assistance our U.S. government provides overseas, both in terms of helping U.S. firms resolve commercial matters and in protecting U.S. citizens overseas. As I'll explain, when our local joint venture partners kidnapped my father in Shanghai, it was the consulate officers who rushed over to the office where he was held to free him.

Back in 1992 when we first entered the Chinese market, we were a typical American small business lured by the siren songs of a billion consumers. Within a few short years, we invested heavily and established a total of eight regional joint venture offices throughout China to not only popularize the de-carbonization concept, but also to educate the consumer about the need for automotive preventative maintenance, which was a novel concept at the time. Although by objective standards we were lucky at first to have some of the most well-connected and influential entities in China as our local partners, after the joint ventures became promising, these relationships became a double-edged sword. To make a very long and complex story short, some of our partners conspired to orchestrate the pirating of the firm's products, the embezzlement of joint funds, fraudulent transfers of joint real estate into personal accounts, falsify documentation, and so on. Within several years, everything that could go wrong for an American small business in China went wrong for us, even before the kidnapping. Despite this, it was still difficult to believe that our joint venture partners were behind the kidnapping.

The kidnapping happened in 1996 after my father left a meeting at the joint venture partner's office. He was taken from the lobby into a waiting vehicle and ultimately to the joint venture offices. He was locked and guarded in one of the internal offices. When the guard was not looking, he found a working telephone and called home to the United States. My mother answered the phone. She heard one sentence—I was kidnapped and held in the office—and the phone went dead.

The guard had discovered the call and pulled the phone line as well as all other outside communication to the offices. My father was then asked to sign a ransom note in the presence of several men, one of whom brandished a knife and told him that if he did not do as they say, that would be his last day alive. I called both the U.S. embassy and the U.S. consulate in Shanghai as soon as my mother told me. Luckily, the consulate officers moved swiftly and got there before he was harmed. We attempted to seek a remedy through the legal system, but when even the justices must pause to weigh their decisions against the repercussions of the wrong doers, there isn't much that we could do other than to chalk it up to experience.

Meanwhile, the culprits made sure I knew that my father was kidnapped so that they could send me the message to get out of China. You might also find this interesting: when we pressed criminal charges against the kidnappers, the court dismissed the charges. It found that the kidnapping was in the court's interpretation "nothing more than a discussion among the parties present" Furthermore, the charges could not stand because my father was not maimed during the ordeal! Local police had custody of the ransom note, obviously the most crucial piece of evidence, where it subsequently and conveniently disappeared.

Sharon: *Well, that is quite a story. I am glad that everything worked out. It now seems mundane to ask my next question, but how well informed were you about commercial lending resources and practices when you started your firm?*

Candace: I did not know much about commercial lending resources when I first got started, as we were able to finance our start-up with our own financial resources.

Sharon: *Have you subsequently utilized external financing to support your export operations?*

Candace: We have utilized conventional bank and credit line financing, but have not looked into any EXIM Bank, nor SBA affiliated lending programs. We are, however, currently evaluating the possibility of venture capital as an alternative to conventional financing.

Sharon: *How much did you know about the mechanics of export operations when you first opened your business and went global?*

Candace: I was somewhat familiar with export documentation and the various types of payment methods available. My parents ran a wholesale gifts and novelty company in the seventies and eighties. I would help with the business after school and during holiday breaks. This was good training for me as I learned firsthand the practicalities of accounting (receivable and payable), customer services (shipping and claims), and documentation (some products were also imported).

Sharon: *How have you managed your home life while traveling and doing business globally?*

Candace: I don't travel as extensively as some of my other colleagues who are engaged in global business. However, running any successful business is very time consuming. In a sense, I am very fortunate, because I am not married and therefore do not have the usual family obligations. I also have a very supportive family, as well as a sister who happens to be an excellent cook. However, there is very little private time. Being the boss at this stage in my life and at this stage in our company's development means that overtime is the norm. When I get home, I use the time after dinner and before bed to catch up on the day's news events, as well as to review trade articles and client documents. While I often have to do work over the weekends, I still have time for fun. Although I am unmarried, I have a stable relationship with someone who has a job that is even more demanding than mine. We have learned to treasure the little time we have together. In fact, running a global business teaches you how to treasure everything more in life. I treasure my friends at home and abroad.

Sharon: *How do you conduct yourself while on the road?*

Candace: About half of my travel is business related and the other half is for my advisory work in trade policy. As my firm's reputation has grown, it has dramatically reduced the need for me to travel as a necessary step to closing a deal. However, regardless of whether I travel for business or to attend policy arenas, I always make sure that I conduct myself professionally. In a male-dominated industry, I think it is important for the female executive to conduct business during business hours and only in a professional setting, being careful not to flirt with male clients. I strongly advise against casual activities with male clients after hours unless in a group activity. More often than not, alcohol and relaxed emotions are involved. Regardless of the venue, if at any time during a meeting, I detect that a male colleague has steered the conversation out of the norm of acceptable professional social behavior, I will immediately steer it back before these exchanges get out of hand.

In general, I am very cautious when I travel alone. I always stay in reputable hotels, take taxis companies that are known to the hotel or to my meeting host, and most often I eat at the hotel or well-established local restaurants nearby, unless I am accompanied by a local. I never go out alone at night. I rather use the time alone at the hotel to organize my notes from the day's meetings and to prepare for the following days. A male colleague once asked me why I would rather pay $20 to park in the hotel lot than at the shopping center a half a block down, which was free to the public. If I knew with certainty that my meetings that day at the hotel would end before sundown, then I would have no problem parking at the free lot. However, since my meeting included a dinner event, I felt that my safety was worth more than the $20 I had to pay for the hotel lot. I also never drink alcoholic beverages when I am away from home. I like to make sure that I always have my wits about me when I am away from home on business, regardless of whether I am alone, or traveling with a colleague. If the situation calls for some champagne or dinner wine, I would take a small sip, so I won't offend the host or attract attention, but never more.

Sharon: *And how did you stay physically fit and manage your weight while on the road?*

Candace: I always have a very full schedule when I travel. Time permitting; I take walks around the hotel and its immediate area for exercise as well as sightseeing. Weight management is not much of a problem at the moment, which became evident when my boyfriend described me as Olive Oyl when he saw me after one of my trips abroad.

Sharon: *You obviously know what you are doing and are very sure-footed. What are the foundations for your self-confidence?*

Candace: My self-confidence is founded on the belief that I know what I am doing. A number of our clients have told us that they find our knowledge of the industry and our products to be very impressive. A few of our most prominent clients have even flat out told us that we take better care of our customers than some of the biggest firms in the industry. It makes our day when a customer calls us for no other reason than to tell us how much they like our product. So the better we take care of our customers, the more confidence we have in our products, our firm, and even in ourselves. Customer endorsements have become the basis of my own self-confidence when I make presentations before prospective clients.

Personal self-confidence, however, has many deep roots. In my case, my family upbringing has had a big and positive influence on my self-confidence and self-worth. My mother is a role model and is a very loving, intelligent, and strong woman. I continue to look to her for guidance and am grateful to her and to my father for instilling in us a very strong moral compass. My philosophy of life has also helped me to feel strong, in that I believe that I am on the right path in life and that I have the right set of values to be happy in life. One such value is that I am not greedy. Yes, I want to be rich, as does my brother. However, neither of us is willing to get rich by unethical means. I am also strengthened by my belief that failure does not equate to character flaw, but rather that it serves as motivation for improvement. I also believe, as do many other Chinese, that success is attributable both to hard work and to luck. Therefore, I work hard to improve my luck. Most importantly, I believe that self-esteem should be derived from pride in one's work and from one's accomplishments. In this regard, I can hold my head high. I also believe that what goes around comes around; therefore, good luck follows those who do good deeds.

Finally, I think it goes without saying that, for a woman, feeling good and looking good are inextricably linked. Therefore, it is important to take good care of oneself and to dress appropriately for the occasion. It is also important to smile, and when you face adversity, to remember to count your blessings first and realize that many things could be worse. Last but not least, for petite women like me, it is important to maintain my good posture and to establish my presence by taking as much room as I need to look and feel at ease.

Sharon: *Upon final reflection, what main advice would you like to give our readers about doing business globally? What are your top ten recommendations?*

Candace: 1. Research the market and be adequately prepared for both the expected and unexpected.

2. Choose one's partners carefully and be sensitive to cultural differences.

3. Be flexible and remember that your customers are your most valuable assets.

4. Always use common sense.

5. Make sure that your expectations are realistic.

6. Makes sure that you are adequately financed, because there is often a lengthy waiting period before one can expect a return on investment.

7. Guard your intellectual property and company secrets. Be cautious of unusual ploys aimed at forcing you to divulge sensitive information.

8. Utilize the resources of the U.S. government, and maintain a good network of both friends and colleagues.

9. Know when to walk away. When all else fails, don't keeping banging your head against the proverbial wall—your time and energy are better spent elsewhere.

10. Don't even think about participating in any get-rich quick schemes, especially those from certain countries we have all heard about. Stick to the letter of the law in the way that all aspects of your business is being conducted, and remember that we all have a responsibility to operate on the right side of the Foreign Corrupt Practices Act and to create a positive example of Americans doing business abroad.

* * *

Cartoonist Draws on R...
Los Kitos Succeed as Creatures With Assimilati...

Martha Montoya
President
Los Kitos

Contact:

Los Kitos
1833 E. 17th Street, Suite 210
Santa Ana, CA. 92705

Phone: (714) 542-7787
Fax (714) 542-7787
Email: martham@loskitos.com
Web: http://www.loskitos.com

Martha Montoya
President and Creator, Los Kitos

Sharon: *Martha, I can only imagine your excitement when you saw Los Kitos (which means little dolls) featured on the first page of the Wall Street Journal; indeed, yours is not a road commonly taken! Your road was long, arduous, and lonely but you hung in there and made your dreams come true. Now, the whole world is smiling with you and Los Kitos. I know that the Pope has even written to you to encourage you keep up the good work with Los Kitos and that your global reach is expanding everyday, even as we speak. I am very grateful to you for caring so much about this book project and for sharing your inspirational story with us. Please tell us about the secrets to your amazing and growing success.*

First, tell us why you wanted to become a business owner and how you got started?

Martha: I started my business because I wanted to be in control of my destiny and to have the ability to respond quickly to demand in the marketplace. Although I am originally from Colombia, I first became a business owner here in America. I did, however, gain relevant business experience in exporting in Colombia prior to moving to America.

As the Wall Street Journal article explained, I have an internationally syndicated cartoon business, based on my comic strip called *Los Kitos*. I own the characters of my comic strip and the associated trademark and copyrights. My company enters into licensing agreements with manufacturers to give them permission to use our comic strip character's images on different consumer products.

Sharon: *What are your comic strip characters about?*

Martha: My characters live in a virtual world that mirrors our own. Hence, their purpose is to share insights about how to live life. For example in one comic strip, one of my favorite characters knocks on a series of doors to find that they are all closed until he gets to the last one. The message is about opportunity: opportunity is not a one-time shot. You have to keep pursuing it until you succeed.

Sharon: *What is the inspiration for your stories and messages?*

Martha: My parents were business owners in Colombia. When I was growing up I observed how my parents managed their business and saw how they solved problems. My characters pass on the lessons I have learned and share their optimism about how to overcome adversity.

Sharon: *How do you measure success in your cartoon business?*

Martha: There are two standard ways of measuring success in this industry. One is from the financial point of view, and the other measure is one's *Q factor*—which measures how well known the characters are. Personally, I considered myself successful as soon as my characters began to be published in newspapers. At that point, I knew that the message my characters carried was being conveyed to the public. This was the most important thing to me, even more important than merely making money. It was also very satisfying to meet people who had read my comic strip and who gleaned its message.

Sharon: *How did you get into the cartoon business?*

Martha: This is a funny story because I cannot draw—in fact, I studied biology and chemistry. Typically, cartoonists are trained artists. In my case, coming from Colombia, being a cartoonist would have been frowned upon. The expectation is that I would have become a doctor or lawyer, certainly not a cartoonist. One is not encouraged to explore and to seek out nontraditional professions. So, privately, and on my own time, I used to draw and create little bubble characters [like *Los Kitos*]. Although I could not draw, I always focused on the eyes and smiles of my characters, as I believe that these are the windows to the souls of the characters. Eventually, I created over 200 distinct characters. This was essentially a lifelong endeavor. I kept drawing my characters until I mastered them. In some ways my lack of technical skill in drawing has been a blessing because I am able to focus on getting my message out.

Sharon: *So you had to learn how to draw and you had to learn about the cartoon industry at the same time.*

Martha: One of the reasons I came to this country was to learn about the business of the cartoon industry. While I was in the process of studying these characters and how their comic strips were created, I also realized that the merchandising aspect of the business was where the real money was made.

Sharon: *How were you able to come to the United States?*

Martha: First, I should tell you that my family owned a private school in Colombia—this was their business. I was involved in the school, taking care of the division for girls. I asked my father if I could run the school one day, but as I had brothers, he favored them to take over the business. As it became clear that my future in my family's business would be marginalized, I started contemplating the possibility of moving to the United States and striking out on my own in business. I asked my father to support me in my move to the United States. As he was not supportive, I decided to get married, in part to get out of the house, and also in part to have someone to support me in the move here.

Sharon: *Did your husband plan to move to the U.S. with you?*

Martha: No, my husband was not interested in emigrating to the United States, although he was interested in traveling to America. Our first visit lasted three weeks, during which time we visited Disneyland—cartoon heaven, from my vantage point. From that moment I began to strategize about how to actually move to the United States. Once we left America we traveled to Australia. My husband wanted to stay there, but I wanted to go to Los Angeles. As we were not getting along, we decided to go our separate ways.

Sharon: *Did you divorce your husband at that point?*

Martha: I would like to take a moment to share something very personal about the break up of my marriage, as I think that it is important for the readers to understand that in life we all have to grow and to evolve. It was a difficult decision to break up with my husband. I think my biggest obstacle was letting go of old traditions about marriage that had become detrimental both to my soul and to my sense of reason. I was brought up to believe that marriage was forever. When I realized that I was in the wrong marriage, I still tried to hold on, despite the fact that the marriage had become seriously dysfunctional, bordering on being physically dangerous for me. Staying in the marriage as long as I did was, to many onlookers, totally inconsistent with my strong personality and innate intelligence. What others could not perceive, however, is that there are many facets that make up our being, intelligence being only one of them. A person's background and traditions equally weigh in to form the total person. In this case, it was necessary for me to extricate myself from my old traditions and from the influences in my life that were causing me to stay in an unhealthy situation. What gave me the inertia to change my situation was catching my husband in bed with another woman. This pushed me over the edge and freed me!

Just as it takes a compelling event to create the inertia and will to change in a personal context, it also takes that in a business context. In the latter regard, however, I was not conflicted and totally focused on developing my business.

Sharon: *How did you go about developing your business once you were free?*

Martha: I went to live in Los Angeles, but I didn't know anyone and I didn't have much money either. So I cleaned houses and baby-sat on a live-in basis. It was a tough job, but I stuck it out for six months. Subsequently, as I was bilingual, I applied for and was accepted for a job working in the library of a junior high School. The year that I worked there enabled me to learn a lot and to spend time learning about the cartoon industry. I researched everything about the cartoon industry from biographies of cartoonist like Hanna-Barbera, to studying about licensing agreements, et cetera.

Sharon: *What was your next move along your critical path to breaking into the cartoon business?*

Martha: I knew from my research that it would cost a lot of money to get into the cartoon business, so I had to begin to earn more money than I did working in the library. My next move was to become a receptionist for an international telecommunication business. Fortunately, within a few months I was promoted to the position of office manager. Eventually, I began to assist the firm in their international business. I was able to do this because I had prior international business exporting flowers from Colombia through which I learned how to organize international shipments, how to manage letters of credit and international payments, and so on.

Sharon: *Tell us more about your international experience in Colombia prior to your move to the United States.*

Martha: I worked in the flower industry in Colombia, facilitating the international shipments of the firm for which I worked. Most of our flowers were shipped via air and were destined for Europe. I worked for this firm from the time I was eighteen years old, and over the years, my responsibilities in the firm grew. I used to visit the flower growers to make sure their parcels were ready for shipment. On the weekends I would handle the paperwork pursuant to the shipment of the goods.

Sharon: *Wasn't this a lot of responsibility at such a young age?*

Martha: It was a lot of responsibility but I was used to pressure and responsibility at an early age. I had contemplated becoming a professional tennis player and was well on my way toward doing so, when in the end I decided not to pursue that career. After my tennis career ended, I fully engaged myself in the flower export business. Although it appears that there may be a disconnect between playing tennis, studying biology, working in the flower industry, and later becoming a cartoonist, in fact, there is a common thread: I have always worked hard, and am extremely disciplined. It is my discipline that has served me well in establishing and growing my cartoon business. Also, my international experience through the flower business also served my cartoon business well by acquainting me with many operational aspects of doing international business. I often draw on the lessons I learned in the flower business in managing the international aspects of my cartoon business. For instance, I learned about the importance of quality control, of properly planning logistics, of making the proper security arrangements, and of the importance of export documentation and financing.

Sharon: *Did your flower company do business on open account?*

Martha: No, never, and I never would. I'd rather sell the goods at a lower price than to take the risk of shipping on open account.

Sharon: *What are some of the other lessons you learned from exporting flowers from Colombia?*

Martha: Because flowers are perishable, you learn that time is of the essence and that all arrangements have to be airtight. From the minute you cut the flower, the game is in play. By contrast, working for a company that exports nonperishable goods is a breeze!

Sharon: *Back to your story about working for the telecommunications company in the United States and helping to facilitate their export operations.*

Martha: My first target in improving their export operations was to look at their logistic arrangements. I was interested, on their behalf, in them getting the goods to the destination faster and getting paid faster, so I investigated alternative shipping routes, also ensuring to choose routes with minimal security risks. My employers were happy with my work and eventually I became the manager of the whole company. My expanded responsibilities included purchasing operations and all aspects of export operations.

Sharon: *How long did you stay with the telecommunications company?*

Martha: I lasted for a year and a half only because I wanted to go faster, to do more, and to more quickly move toward my goal of having my own cartoon strip. I decided to get into the frozen food industry, but not the perishable field because I still didn't feel comfortable with the U.S. regulations or with the structure of the U.S. domestic market. It is important to note that, once again, I started at the bottom. I got a job as a receptionist in a frozen food company, knowing that I would be able to work my way up. Besides, while I was serving as a receptionist and had a lot of extra time on the job, I wrote stories for my cartoon characters and integrated things in the stories that I saw around me. For instance, one of my characters worked in the mailroom and knew everything that was going on in the company—art imitating life, no doubt.

The way I penetrated the upper echelon of the frozen fruit company was by getting involved in the company's sourcing operations. My particular forte' was negotiating prices; it is our culture in Colombia to bargain. So, if a supplier quoted his price at $1.10 per kilogram, I would intercede and negotiate a price of $1.05.

Sharon: *Why did upper management let you get involve with their export business when you were merely a receptionist?*

Martha: My advantage was my ability to speak Spanish. From there I was gradually able to go a step further and show what I could do. I was being called on not only for my knowledge of the language, but also for my knowledge of Latin American culture. Part of this cultural awareness was knowing that if suppliers were asking for $1.10, you don't give them their price; instead you start bargaining at $1.00. Furthermore, you have to give them some time to engage in the negotiation. You can't just say here is the new price—take it or leave it. And you have to give them the impression that you will also be giving them some room to negotiate. My chemistry background was also a tremendous help to me in the frozen food business. It enabled me to understand issues pertaining to quality control and to be able to go into factories in different countries and assess their level of quality control. After I figured out this industry it was time to move on.

I was approached by a company in the food industry that supplied foodstuffs to institutions throughout the United States. The company had heard about my experience in sourcing. As they had only sourced their products domestically, they brought me on board to begin to source products internationally. I built an international division for the company and eventually went into business for myself, buying the products on my own account from Latin America and selling them directly to buyers in the United States. For the first time, I started making real money. The first product I bought for my own account was asparagus, from Peru and Ecuador. Next, I focused on mangoes, buying them in season respectively from Peru, Brazil, and Venezuela. As I became known throughout the food industry, I soon received requests from other firms to source everything from produce to fruit. I spent four years doing this business, which was very frenetic and totally time consuming. However, I still had Los Kitos on my mind.

Sharon: *When did you begin your cartoon business?*

Martha: After four years in the purchasing business I was almost ready to start my cartoon business. First, I had to do a few more deals. I got married again, had a baby, and bought my last big shipment of mangos before I left sourcing business. It is a funny story about what happened with my last big purchasing deal, which helped push me over the edge to start my own business. I was eight months pregnant and in the middle of a large, $20 million mango transaction. The mangos were being sourced from Peru; however, they had to be transported over land through Ecuador, where they would be subsequently loaded onto a banana boat. A fight erupted between Ecuador and Peru, so this transportation route proved to be unfeasible. Although eight months pregnant, I had to jump on an airplane and work out an alternative transportation plan. Although everything worked out in the end, I decided that enough was enough and that it was time to start my own cartoon business.

In 1995 I finally established Los Kitos. I initially worked out of my home and spent a lot of time drawing my characters, getting my stories together, and reflecting on my previous business experiences and to figure out how to apply the lessons I learned. The first lesson I reflected upon was the importance of public relations. I had previous experience in creating small marketing campaigns in the food business. For instance, I designed the boxes for our fruit, our labels, and helped with the marketing strategies. I drew on this experience to create the logo and other promotional materials for Los Kitos.

Sharon: *Did you have any employees or help in getting started in your business?*

Martha: At first, I used college interns; they were fresh and enthusiastic and had a lot of good ideas. They helped me formulate my business plan and helped me in researching the market pursuant to marketing comic strips.

Sharon: *After you figured out your business plan and developed your portfolio, how did your business actually take off—what is the first deal you made?*

Martha: As we were selling a comic news strip, our goal was to get the strip into newspapers.

Sharon: *Were you focused on the domestic market at this point?*

Martha: Initially we only focused on the domestic market. Our specific goal was to get placed in the number one Hispanic newspaper in the country, which is *La Opinion* in Los Angeles. It was important for us to start at the top because we knew if we cracked this one, others would follow. After around four months of persistent marketing, we were successful and got into the newspaper. It was at a time when I was struck down with appendicitis. Fortunately, I had created enough material for the strip to be able to run with the material I had already prepared.

Once in the newspaper, my hardest challenge was being able to detach myself from criticism. As you have seen, it was such a hard road to come to this point. Each character was like a child of mine, and it was hard to accept criticism of my "babies." Interestingly, I recently learned that "Snoopy" creator Charles Schultz said that Snoopy was him. I felt a bit like this too. Philosophically, the big issue is one's attitude about winning and losing. It is hard to be in business and believe that you will be a winner and then you lose something. Reconciling one's views about winning and losing is a very important lesson in life. It is especially important when what you are selling is "you," in the way that Charles Schultz meant it when he said that Snoopy was himself.

I have had many occasions when I had to put my philosophy to work and learn how to distance myself from criticism. Five months after we got into *La Opinion*, the next newspaper we approached rejected my comic strip, saying that my characters looked like little Chinese fortune cookies and that he did not like them. This broke my heart, and I was sad for about a week before I could pull myself together again. In pulling myself up again, I remembered when I was selling produce and one potential buyer would say that he didn't like the tomatoes because they were too green. I did not hesitate to move on to find a buyer who did like our tomatoes. Similarly, in this case, I realized that one person's opinion does not necessarily reflect everyone's in the market. So I learned how to press on and go to the next buyer!

Sharon: *Was it difficult to accept the opinions and input of your employees in developing the cartoon strip?*

Martha: Frankly, it has been difficult. I have had to grow into being able to accept the design inputs of others.

Sharon: *Take us through the steps of going global with Los Kitos.*

Martha: My first task in my strategy to go global with Los Kitos was to find distributors in target overseas markets. The big issue for my business is the collection of the money from the newspaper in which the comic strip runs. Initially, I did not know how the international syndication game worked. A friend of mine from Universal Press explained to me that the domestic syndicates deal with "master syndicators" who, in turn, distribute the material on a worldwide basis. This business is handled through syndication licensing agreements. These master syndicators have a catalog of the properties they are distributing, such as Garfield, Snoopy, Cathy, and so on. They make a judgment call on which comic strips are appropriate for which markets, in view of local cultural norms. There are about three or four international syndicators, and seven or eight domestic syndicators.

Sharon: *Would you have figured this out on your own?*

Martha: It would have taken me a long to time to discover how the market works. Fortunately, my friend from Universal Press distributes the Garfield cartoon strip. He liked Los Kitos and felt that it did not pose any competition to his market segment. So he became a mentor and showed me the way to get into international syndication.

Sharon: *Why did you want to go global with Los Kitos?*

Martha: As Los Kitos is in Spanish; our domestic distribution is limited to the Spanish language newspapers in the major urban areas with large Hispanic populations. We are featured in all of the major Spanish-language newspapers but have found that mainstream newspapers in the U.S. market have thus far failed to embrace our Spanish-language comic strip and to incorporate it into the mainstream market. We believed, therefore, that in order to grow, we had to branch out into foreign markets.

Sharon: *How many newspapers is Los Kitos featured in at present?*

Martha: We are featured in 305 newspapers all together, including our presence in foreign newspapers in such countries as Switzerland, France, the Dominican Republic, Brazil, India, and others.

Sharon: *How did you get started in getting Los Kitos featured in Spanish-language newspapers in the United States?*

Martha: I actually cold-called the newspapers directly. I explained what our comic strip is about and encouraged their interest to include it. This, of course, was not easy, I had to sell them on the idea and ensure that they understood my vision for the strip.

Sharon: *Was the fact that Los Kitos was featured in so many U.S. newspapers a major selling point with overseas newspapers?*

Martha: Absolutely. Without such U.S. market penetration the foreign newspapers would not have even talked to me. I did my research before contacting the different overseas newspapers and knew that they viewed the Spanish language newspaper market in the U.S. to be an "overseas market." This made it easier for them to believe that their markets would also positively respond to the comic strip.

Sharon: *Did you join a syndicate or continue to represent your comic strip yourself?*

Martha: One of the largest syndicates handling comic strips in America took us on and helped place us in foreign newspapers all over the world, from China to the Ukraine. Can you believe that we get over fifty hits per day on our electronic version of our comic strip from the Ukraine?

Sharon: *Do you put your comic strip on a website in addition to being in various newspapers?*

Martha: Yes, we are on the web at <www.loskitos.com>. Our foreign readers access Los Kitos both from their native language newspapers, where our comic strip is presented both in Spanish and in the local language, and via our website. They come to know about our website from the information about our strip that is disseminated by our syndicate and licensees at trade shows around the world. The beauty of the Internet is that interested parties who cannot access our strip in their local newspaper can visit our website and access our strip directly. This is the power of technology.

Sharon: *Do you collect information from your website that helps you to plan your comic strip?*

Martha: We carefully review our site statistics and know therefore how many hits we are getting from each country and what they are viewing. We use this information to develop and target our strip. We want to underscore for the readers that going digital goes hand in hand with going global. In our case, we are able to gauge consumer response and to glean valuable information—a better method than conducting a survey. For instance, we know which parts of our comic strip are getting the most hits and therefore know what the public likes. Having a website expands our audience in ways we could not have anticipated. For instance, we have gotten letters from inmates at prison, and even from the Pope, on the other end of the scale.

Sharon: *Has the fact that your comic strip is not in English been a constraint?*

Martha: I felt adamant when I started out that my strip should be in Spanish. Many people, even my first licensing agent, thought I was doing the wrong thing and discouraged me. However, I hung in there. And now that there is greater awareness, both locally and internationally, about the importance of the Hispanic segment of the U.S. population, my steadfastness has been rewarded and there is more interest than ever in our Spanish-language comic strip.

Sharon: *Did you have any concerns about the universality of the message or concern about how to translate the message into different languages?*

Martha: I had a great deal of concern. To minimize the problem of translation, I ensure that my strip focuses on action panels rather than words. My readers can fill in their own words based on the action in the strip.

Sharon: *Now let's get down to the money aspect of this deal. How do you really make money?*

Martha: The money is made off the licensing agreements. It is possible to obtain a license to put our characters on various consumer products such as apparel, footwear, and coffee mugs. In order to do this business we use licensing agents who get a cut on the deal, for instance, 35-40 percent. When I started with my first agent around five years ago, this agent only brought us one deal. The agent explained to me that no one understood the characters and how to market and use them. The agent and I amicably agreed to go our separate ways. Subsequently, I established my own in-house licensing department. The challenge of this department is not only to sign up deals for licensing, more importantly its chief mission is to monitor the business under the agreements. This is not an easy task, I can tell you. We engaged a lawyer to develop some model licensing agreements, including such data as how many readers we have in different markets and other aspects of our presence in the different markets. What we wanted to convey to our licensees is that if you want to sell more of your products, use our Los Kitos characters to do so.

As we developed our licensing department, eventually we were able to sign up manufacturing representatives. It became the job of these representatives to sell our characters so that they could be showcased on various manufactured consumer products. Our only limitation in this aspect of our business is that we are not on television yet. For our part, we purposefully wanted to focus on print because this segment of the market is the most loyal of all customers. In addition, we have seen many cases, such as that of the Ninja turtle, where television exposure comes and goes and with it goes the characters. We are in this business for the long run, however. Our aim is to have Los Kitos be a part of the world society. We don't want it to be a fad—we want to be like Snoopy.

Sharon: *How did you learn about the licensing game?*

Martha: We joined the Licensing Industry Marketing Association (LIMA), which gave us access to licensing agents around the world. These agents helped open a new world to us of licensing possibilities such as hair clips for girls, underwear for kids, and many other products we would not have imagined as licensing candidates.

Sharon: *How do you ensure that your characters are being represented as you intended?*

Martha: Our licensees are well known throughout the industry and handle big properties like Barbie, Snoopy, Teletubbies. This does not mean, however, that these manufacturers who are using your characters always abide by the terms of the contract. They might, for instance, agree to manufacture one million socks and instead manufacture two million. Of course, the contract with the manufacturer stipulates that the firm's production can be audited at any time. Indeed, I have been engaged in some audits, but frankly, it is very hard to monitor. We have a "watchdog" firm on retainer that conducts the necessary audits on our behalf. This is standard industry practice, and our contract with manufacturers stipulates that we have the right to conduct such audits.

Sharon: *In how many countries do you have manufacturer licensees through manufacturing representatives?*

Martha: We have fourteen different countries involved with us for different categories of licensing agreements. It is important to note that our domestic licensees in the United States may also obtain rights to sell the products in foreign markets. In order to do this the U.S. firm takes a master license with our firm, and their affiliates overseas take a subsidiary license to their master license. This is a difficult business to manage because we do not want to disturb our other licensing arrangements, nor do we want to give away hot markets prematurely. Needless to say, we negotiate the Master and subsidiary licenses very carefully for each market.

Sharon: *What hot licensing prospects do you see for foreign markets in future?*

Martha: We are excited about the prospects for animation in future. In order to leave enough room for our animation studio to recover its investment, we have to leave certain markets open. For instance, licensing agreements for plush toys in Europe have not been signed, as we consider this to be a very lucrative market that we want to hold for animation investors.

Sharon: *Are you already in the process of developing animation, and if so, do you own your own studios or do you have other licensing agreements with animators?*

Martha: We have two licensing agreements with animation studios; one is with the *Cine Groupe* of Canada for worldwide Internet animation, and another is with the Krislin Entertainment Group in Hollywood for broadcast rights and distribution overseas. Two years ago, there was only one type of animation, broadcast animation (television, video, movies animation). Now there is separate animation for the Internet. Although we license the animation rights, we retain certain creative rights and control all aspects of character development.

Sharon: *To what extent have you involved lawyers in business?*

Martha: I would say that in almost every case we get a lawyer involved in developing and reviewing our various contracts. Some of these contracts are fifty pages long, and each paragraph has to be carefully reviewed.

Sharon: *Do you manufacture any products and sell them directly overseas?*

Martha: We do not manufacture and believe, to the contrary, that the money is in the end of the business we are in, namely licensing. Furthermore, our characters run a broad range of products from toys to clothing to books. It is not necessarily beneficial to specialize; we simply want to ensure that our characters are well established so we can increase the price of our license.

Sharon: *It sounds like you are in the smart part of the business. In closing, what advice would you leave the audience with about how to make their dreams come true?*

Martha: Have a goal and stick to it. And then, to implement the vision, start looking for the right mentors right away. In addition, research, research, and research. I read a book a week, for instance. I read everything about the industry. I also attend many trade shows, and it is through these shows that I have been able to identify who the key players are in the industry and whom I want to approach to be a mentor. I spotted my main mentor, Gary Selvaggio, at a trade show ten years ago, even before I was in the industry. When I was ready I went to him and asked for his help. He gave it freely and has been instrumental in my success in later years.

Sharon: *How do you measure your success today, and how will you measure it in the future?*

Martha: I want to bring joy to others, and I want people to smile. When I get a letter from the Pope or from a prisoner telling me to keep up the good work, then I know that I am on the right track. My characters are doing their job well!

Such satisfaction means more than money. Thinking back on the time when bankers told me that they could not understand the potential of my business because it was intangible, I think, yes, they were right in some way. Indeed, the happiness my characters bring is intangible. But on the other hand, when we sign our licensing agreements and get our royalties in advance, this is tangible. Today, we have no need for external financing, as our royalties are sufficient. But even more rewarding than our royalties is the smiles we bring.

* * *

Gisele Rufer
President
Delance

Contact:

Delance

201 Rte-Principale
CH 2532 Macolin, Switzerland

Phone: (41-32) 323-6401
Fax (41-32) 323-6827
Email: delance@bielstar.ch
Web: http://www.delance.com

«L'excellence au féminin»

Gisèle Rufer is a woman of the new millennium, a sophisticated blend of determination, intelligence and femininity. With degrees in artistic education and engineering, this French-born innovator worked many years for some of the most well-known Swiss watch companies.

During this time, however, a passion burned within to create a truly unique timepiece. So, six years ago, at age 48, Gisele decided to transform her dream into a reality.

Her new company, **DELANCE** Swiss Watches, began creating timepieces exclusively for today's woman. Unlike any in the world, these elegant watches combine exquisite French design with high-precision Swiss craftsmanship. In just a few short years, they have become a talisman, or if you will, a **«TALISWOMAN»** for femininity. The subtle symbolism of the intricately hand-carved gold or steel case represents life, energy and harmony. For Gisele Rufer, her new watches epitomize «Time for Women». They are feminine and subtly powerful... like those who wear them.

Something More...

many women cherish the **DELANCE** watch simply for its elegant beauty, distinctive originality, high quality and raceful prestige. Others appreciate the subtle symbolism it evokes. With its flowing form, the **DELANCE** timepiece reflects the universal symbols of life and harmony.

More than a beautiful jewel...

The diamond shape of the carefully hand-sculpted case represents life. The spiral at 12 o'clock depicts water, the source of all life... the feminine. At 6 o'clock, the cabochon portrays fire or energy... the masculine. Together they trace out the sign of infinity binding the two together in eternal harmony.

The DELANCE watch Perfect Ten, decorated with ten diamonds, was created so that everybody should have the chance to say to a woman: You are perfect, I love you the way you are.

For the woman who receives it, this watch will be an unforgettable present telling her every minute that, at least for one person, she has the best mark – a ten.

The **DELANCE «Perfect Ten»** is set with ten pure Top Wesselton diamonds. The watch is made of 18 carat gold or steel.
The strap is exchangeable and one can choose satin, alligator, steel, silver or gold versions.
The photo depicts a watch with a steel casing and a sterling silver bracelet.

The **DELANCE** watch is 100% Swiss made, with a manual Piguet or ETA quartz movement, a screw-on bottom and an unscratchable sapphire glass. It is water-resistant to a depth of 30 m and has a two year guarantie

To show its solidarity with women around the world, **DELANCE** participate in the Women's World Summit Foundation, an organization helping women in developing nations to create their own businesses.

For other models in the **DELANCE** collection, please visit our website: http://www.delance.com
Photos of G. Rufer available at http://www.gerberstephane.ch

DELANCE
SWISS WATCHES

201 Route Principale CH-2532 Macolin Tél. ++41 32 323 64 01 Fax ++41 32 323 68 27
E-mail: delance@bielstar.ch www.delance.com

Gisele Rufer
President, Delance

Sharon: *Gisele, I believe that you are the only woman in Switzerland who has ever received the prestigious Swiss Oscar Idea award. I know how much this award means to you because you have pioneered in the Swiss watch industry to create special watches for women. When I first met you at the Business Women's Network (BWN) I was really taken with your passion about Delance watches for women. When I learned that you had received the Swiss Idea Oscar, I knew that I had to include you in this book, as I always wanted to interview an Oscar winner. Tell us the secret to your success and how you got started in the watch business.*

Gisele: I have worked in the watch industry for a long time. I was formerly a product manager at Omega watches, where I was in charge of a number of their collections. The Omega collection did not include a watch for women and eventually it became my goal to create one. Omega gave me carte blanche to accomplish this feat. But after spending two or three years of work on the endeavor, I came to the conclusion that Omega did not really want this product.

Sharon: *Was the problem the design of the watch or the firm's lack of commitment to the market segment?*

Gisele: They lacked the commitment to the women's market. They did not believe that it would be profitable enough. At this point, I decided that I had a new calling: to design and manufacture a special watch for women on my own.

Sharon: *Why do you think that it was your destiny to manufacture a watch?*

Gisele: When I was growing up, I always had a vision that someday I would make something special for women, but I didn't know what. My father died when I was only seven years old. Consequently, my mother, who had five small children, had to work to earn a living. She is now seventy-five years old and still runs a shop selling decorative ornaments such as porcelain and crystal. Because she was a foreigner in Switzerland, it was difficult for her to find employment. She adapted economically by becoming an entrepreneur. She has always been my role model, not only for her successes in business but also for the example she set as a beautiful, kind, and vivacious woman.

Like my mother, I found my *raison d'etre* through entrepreneurship. It took me a while to connect with my entrepreneurial spirit, but when I did, I was consumed by it. My business is me—I had to start my business to fully realize myself and lifelong goals.

Sharon: *What are some of the impressions about growing up that influenced your decision to become an entrepreneur and exporter?*

Gisele: It was always my impression that there are so many marvelous women all over the world, women like my mother, who are so talented and multifaceted, yet who are unknown. I wanted to make something for women that expressed their strength and their eternity. I did not know exactly how to accomplish this until I realized that a watch would be the perfect symbol, one that expresses the value of time for women. My goal, therefore, was to create a watch for all of the creative, intelligent, and strong women all over the world that expressed both their strength and their eternity. I designed the watch to symbolize these attributes of women and call it the Delance Eternity Watch.

Sharon: *Your product was conceived as a global product then, correct?*

Gisele: Absolutely. I couldn't make much of a business out of targeting the Swiss market, could I? Seriously, I think if you create your business and if you want to be global, you have to think globally from the very beginning. When you think globally, you have to use a language that is understood all over the world. Whereas music is inherently international, as is dance, it was more of a challenge for me to create a universally understood "language" for my watch. I created this bridge through shaping my watch into a well-known, ancient symbol of eternity. This symbol is easily recognized and universally understood by women, as well as men, all over the world.

Sharon: *What were the first steps you took in starting your global business? Once you had settled on the idea, how did you proceed to create your global enterprise?*

Gisele: My first step was to get in touch with women all over the world. I traveled extensively to meet women and asked them to define *time*. Interestingly, the most frequently cited answer among the women from around the world was that *time is life*! They expressed this by saying that as we give our time to raise our families, and as we are the givers, organizers, and managers of life—time is life! Not one woman said that time is money.

Sharon: *I bet men would have said that time is money.*

Gisele: Women do not measure the value of time in dollars and cents; this is not the value women give to their time. When I asked women what is important in their lives and in the way they spend their time and what they are struggling for, their unanimous answer was that they are striving for harmony. And when I read your story, Sharon, I think it's the same for you. Women want to be in a harmonious state with everything in their lives. A lot of women also said that they wanted something more than just than everyday life—something spiritual. Therefore, in addition to capturing the strength and eternity of women, I also wanted my watch to capture the sentiments of life, harmony, and spirituality. This is why I chose the diamond shape for my watches, because it symbolizes life and harmony.

Sharon: *After you interviewed women about their goals, what did you do next to ascertain how women would react to your watches?*

Gisele: My next step was to survey women to ascertain whether they would purchase a high quality watch that did not have a famous label. Some said no, and I knew that they were not my clients. Many, however, said that they would buy the kind of special watch we designed if they loved the watch or if there was a special reason to buy the watch. My challenge was to satisfy these potential customers by making a watch that was very beautiful and recognizable at first sight, and that made each woman feel that the watch was made just for her.

Sharon: *Gisele, it seems that you started out being very certain about the market potential for this product. Why is it that Omega, to whom you gave the idea to first for the watch, did not come to the same conclusions about the market potential for the watch? What made you think that you knew better than Omega?*

Gisele: I must say that I didn't have a very good opinion of the men who decided that there was not a market for women. I thought that they were flat-out wrong in their judgment. Ten years later, of course, they have changed their minds. My goal was to create my watch, and going into to business was the way to accomplish this. Frankly, I wanted to create a watch, not a company. However, once I became an entrepreneur, I felt that I was born with an entrepreneurial spirit. Sometimes it takes external forces to activate the latent entrepreneurial spirit. For many women, this moment of inertia occurs when they reach the glass ceiling in their jobs. In my case, the desire to create a special watch for women is the inertia that pushed me forward.

Sharon: *Why couldn't you get somebody else to make your watch?*

Gisele: I could not do it that way; this product is connected with who I am. Besides, I was the only woman in the Swiss watch industry with the stature to get this product made. I am a pioneer in the Swiss watch industry, and the only female Swiss watchmaker who is making watches that capture the spirit of women.

Sharon: *Tell us more about how you planned this global venture.*

Gisele: Once I clarified and refined my design concept and target market, my next step was to identify all of the pros and cons of embarking upon this global venture. The pros included that I am an engineer, an artist, and I can speak at least three languages very well. In addition, I have the resources and connections to travel all over the world, and I am a good communicator and a good saleswoman. Moreover, I am well known in the watch industry and am famous for having launched the *Flik-Flak* watch during my tenure as product manager for Omega.

Sharon: *What about the cons?*

Gisele: In Switzerland, men between the ages of thirty-five and forty are responsible for most new business start-ups. It is quite unusual for a woman of my age, forty-eight years old at the time, to venture out to start a business on her own. Thus, I first had to cross an internal psychological boundary to refrain from feeling that my age was a disadvantage. To the contrary, I decided that it was an advantage, bringing with it maturity, experience, and my well-established name in the watch industry. In terms of external constraints, the problem was that I did not have adequate financing to establish my new business.

Sharon: *How did you organize financing for your global venture?*

Gisele: Although I had no money, I had connections. So my strategy was to go as far as I could without having to obtain formal financing. I engaged a network of friends, family, and business partners to invest in my venture. In addition, I was able to self-finance part of the venture and drew on the knowledge I had gleaned from my mother, who was also a financial planner, on how to structure financing. At the same time, I was selected by the Genilem Foundation of Geneva, which mentors new start-up companies, to receive some start-up capital.

Sharon: *Did you also approach venture capital companies to seek financing?*

Gisele: In Switzerland, we do not have a mature venture capital industry. Ultimately, I had to approach traditional banks.

Sharon: *When you approached the banks, did you give them your business plan, and had you already designed the watch?*

Gisele: I had a detailed business plan that I shared with potential financiers. But when I showed them the plan—and when I shared my vision that my watch would express life, harmony, and spirituality—they were incredulous. They could not believe that I could accomplish this feat, especially when Omega could not. When I first showed them my business plan, I didn't have a prototype of the watch to convince them, so they were reluctant to provide financing. In the end, I could not wait, as I had waited over forty years to realize my goals. So I decided to self-finance the project.

I could go far because I made a few pieces and sold them and used the money from these sales to finance on-going operations. Now, however, I need more money to go further and to grow my business. Specifically, I need to invest more in marketing, in distribution, and in overhead to pay employees, et cetera. My representative here, for example, gets paid very little—as she is investing in Delance as one of its ambassadors; however, we at least need to pay her expenses.

Sharon: *But manufacturing watches is a very expensive proposition, isn't it? How much do your watches cost?*

Gisele: My watches cost from $750 to $65,000. The price goes up depending upon how the watch is customized with diamonds as accents. The watch I am wearing, for instance, has three rows of diamonds and costs $25,000.

Sharon: *Did you have any business or management training prior to running your own company?*

Gisele: I felt that I needed more business preparation, so I went back to university, for six months, to obtain a degree in entrepreneurship.

Sharon: *Do you have any special strategies for hiring and managing staff?*

Gisele: Remember, I had a social goal as well as a business goal in terms of what I wanted to accomplish with my watches. Just as I wanted my watches to express the excellence of women, I also wanted to engage all women in the production and execution of my watch business. The women who work with me share my dreams, and we work harmoniously together.

Sharon: *What stage are you at currently? Do you have adequate financing to grow your business?*

Gisele: Not yet. My strategy is to find female entrepreneurs, as partners, all over the world who are in a position to both invest and launch Delance in their respective countries.

Sharon: *You mean you want to have Delance China, Delance Japan, and so on?*

Gisele: Yes, this is exactly what I want, and even more. My dream is to find Delance ambassadors in different towns around the world. They would be women who understand the product, identify with the message it conveys, and who would be willing to market the watches to retail outlets in their areas. In addition, they might also employ a strategy of private distribution, wherein they would market through a series of private gatherings and workshops on women's topics. Of course, they would wear the watch while so doing, as one picture is worth a thousand words. This could also be done in coordination with retail shops with which they form a strategic alliance in their areas.

My role continuing role would be to become a motivational speaker at the promotional events organized by Delance Ambassadors. I would also continue to forge strategic alliances with big corporations like DuPont, Merrill Lynch, and Citibank in order to entice them to give the watch away as a corporate gift to valued customers and employees.

Right now, I am the main ambassador of Delance. As such, I am often called upon to speak at women's gatherings. I use these occasions to recruit new Delance ambassadors. I am on the lookout for other ambassadors—perhaps you included, Sharon. Here is a deal: If this book is successful, you must buy a Delance, and when people ask you about your watch, you must tell them the Delance story.

Sharon: *Some women are reluctant to be salespersons. But if they are connected to the product in some way then they are not selling—they are networking, right?*

Gisele: Right, but there are also opportunities for them to become indirect salespersons by enlisting others who would sell it directly or by marshaling publicity for the product. As I said in the beginning, when I did my initial marketing, women said they would buy an expensive watch from a not-well-known watchmaker only if there were something special about the watch or if there were a special reason to buy the watch. The reason to buy this watch is that is made by women for women to symbolize womanhood. Furthermore, the watch can be customized to symbolize a special occasion. For instance, if you have been married for ten years, then you can put ten diamonds on the watch. Or the watch can signify eternity because of its design, which incorporates the symbol for infinity.

Sharon: *Are you ever overwhelmed by the scale of your own investment and about the risks inherent in your venture?*

Gisele: Sometimes I am overwhelmed, but I just have to manage. I can lose money but I can never lose the benefits that I have gained through trying to make my dreams come true.

There is a distinction between being afraid of risks and being a fearful person in general. I am not a fearful person. I do have questions, however, and I also have had difficult moments, such as when I was robbed of my watches in Switzerland. Also, every time I go through customs it is a toss of the dice. Even when everything is in order, something could still go wrong. I do not have fear in an unwarranted way, however. Whenever something happens, I try to find a solution. One's willingness to take risks has to do with the way they were raised. Both of my parents were entrepreneurs. I saw my parents take risks, and as a consequence, I am not afraid of risks, even though the level of risk in my particular business is quite high. It is clear that I am under pressure to sell my watches, given the level of investment involved in this business. Yet I am not afraid, as I am sure that I will succeed.

Sharon: *Do you do often seek advice as a way of lowering your risks?*

Gisele: I take advice when I need it. Like you, however, I have a great deal of self-confidence. My mother was a woman who could show me the way. She was an entrepreneur, and I wanted to be at least as good as her. I love people and they love me back, so I feel well supported and happy. This creates a positive framework for working with others. I love the process of sitting around a table and having everyone contribute their ideas and their enthusiasm to what we are trying to accomplish. Through such processes we are able to create products that are at the highest level of excellence. So, I am always receptive to good ideas, and I integrate them with my own. In my own company, for instance, I have created nothing. I just opened my eyes and looked around me and took what I could take and combined it, working with our production and design specialists. Seeking advice on how to run my business, however, is where I draw the line, as I am trailblazing and creating a new path in the watch industry where others have not been.

Sharon: *Do you make a distinction between creative advice and technical advice?*

Gisele: Yes, what I typically seek is technical advice. For instance, I have sought technical advice to create my CD-ROM. I have given my ideas about the content and look and feel of the presentation to the technical experts but have left it up to them to configure the product.

Sharon: *Did you seek advice on whether you should go into business in the first place?*

Gisele: No—remember that my bosses at Omega said that there was no market for a woman's watch of the caliber I had in mind. Therefore, I neither respected nor agreed with their advice. But I did ask salespeople in the jewelry business what their clientele wanted and told me that there was always the room for anything women want.

Sharon: *Do you seek advice about business strategies?*

Gisele: Yes, right now we are taking advice on whether we should try to sell our watches through E-commerce. I am going to a conference soon of Swiss watchmakers to examine whether high-quality expensive watches can be sold on the Internet.

Sharon: *What were some of your biggest strategic decisions when you started out?*

Gisele: One of my first big strategic considerations was the name of the product. I wanted to be sure the name had a positive connotation and positive sound in every language. For instance, names with the letter *r* are difficult to pronounce in many languages, so I wanted to avoid such names. I wanted the name to be soft for women, to be lyrical, and to be French. I tried to invent a name combining letters. But then it came to me. My father, whose name was Delance, was making watches when he died at thirty-two years old. As I was only seven years old when he died, I felt like he died without saying goodbye. I decided to include my father's name in a long list of names that I faxed to women all over the world. Surprisingly, Delance was the name that was the first choice of the women surveyed. Hence, I chose this name for my company, and in the process I was re-connected to my father. The funny thing is that although my watch is made by women for women, it has my father's name. In the end, I think this is good because the watch's design incorporates the concept of the inseparability of men and women.

Sharon: *Did you give special planning consideration to the aspect of packaging?*

Gisele: Just as I care about the excellence of my product, I also care about its packaging. I wanted to ensure that its packaging reflected our high standards, so I decided to have creative packaging that was reusable. Accordingly, we use a piece of fabric that the watch rests on in a beautiful little box. The fabric can be used as a hair ribbon, and the box can also be reused.

Sharon: *When all is said and done, do you consider that your firm has been successful in the export arena? If so, how do you define success?*

Gisele: I define success in increments and in many steps. For me, a success is something that makes me happy when I believe that I am nearest to my goal. I would never claim to swim in success, however, as I never know what tomorrow will bring. When I won the Swiss Idea Oscar this year I certainly felt like I was on the right track. As you know, it is the first time this prize has been awarded to a woman for having a special idea. My special idea was to create a watch that expressed time in a global way and not in a linear way. Usually, watches merely express the time in hours, minutes, and seconds. By contrast, my watch is designed to express a spiritual value of time.

Sharon: *Do you have a quantitative measure of success for your business?*

Gisele: When we have sold ten thousand watches, and when the name Delance is as familiar as Omega and women are rushing out to buy it, then we can rest on our laurels. In the meantime, I am looking for women investors all over the world to help launch the product. I need the women in China. I need the women in Japan, women in the United States, and all over.

Sharon: *What strategies are you pursuing to identify these women?*

Gisele: I am networking constantly, traveling from one part of the world to the other to participate in conferences as a speaker to tell the story of my watches. In the process, I am increasing my recognition by my peers in the watch industry, and I am beginning to motivate women to become Delance ambassadors around the world. In the meantime, we are developing our business strategy to enable our strategic partners and ambassadors to tailor their business arrangements with Delance in the way that works best with their sales and marketing strategies. We are working through this right now with our first U.S.-based Delance ambassador, Pamela Mattson, in Atlanta.

Sharon: *You are working very hard at making your business a success. How are you balancing your hard work with other parts of your life?*

Gielse: My intensive travel schedule limits my social life. I barely have time for my family when it is time to plan another trip. I look upon this as a temporary situation, however; it is another investment I have to make in getting my business off the ground.

Sharon: *What about some of the off-setting social benefits you derived from traveling?*

Gisele: I have friends in all cities around the worlds—look at my address book. As you can see, I have a list of friends here in Washington, D.C., and in many other places. I send my friends emails, advising them when I am going to be in town and how to contact me.

Sharon: *I also have many friends around the world, but, in my view, this is a good news and bad news story. Sometimes I want to share something with a particular person, but that person is not near me and I feel a little sad. That is the bad news. On the positive side, I am grateful to have so many friends around the world. How do you feel about this?*

Gisele: I feel exactly the same way, but I try to manage process of staying in touch electronically by saying a few words but letting them know that I am thinking about them. My daughter lives in California, and the rest of my family lives in other countries. We do not see each other often, but we are able to stay connected electronically, at least.

Sharon: *How do you achieve harmony in your life?*

Gisele: Harmony starts within one's own self. It demands that you take care of yourself and that you do the things that are right for yourself. It is only when this is accomplished that you can be in harmony with others. There is both a spiritual dimension of being right with oneself and a physical dimension; regarding the latter, I strive to stay fit to meet the rigors and demands of foreign travel.

Sharon: *In order to be successful in business, you have to be successful in life. You must stay in balance and in harmony with all of the parts of your life. Do you agree?*

Gisele: You cannot be successful for long if you are not in harmony. You will break down one day. In French, we say: *"Qui veut aller loin ménage sa monture,"* which means "The one who wants to ride a long way, must take care of his horse." I am my horse!

            I would also like to share a poem that I recently read by Erma Bombeck that similarly speaks to the issue of taking care of one's horse.

IF I HAD MY LIFE TO LIVE OVER
by Erma Bombeck

I would have talked less and listened more.

I would have invited friends over to dinner even if the carpet was stained and the sofa faded.

I would have eaten the popcorn in the "GOOD" living room and worried much less about the dirt when someone wanted to light a fire in the fireplace.

I would have taken the time to listen to my grandfather ramble about his youth.

I would never have insisted the car windows be rolled up on a summer day because my hair had just been teased and sprayed.

I would have burned the pink candle sculpted like a rose before it melted in storage.

I would have sat on the lawn with my children and not worried about grass stains.

I would have cried and laughed less while watching television and more while watching life.

I would have gone to bed when I was sick instead of pretending the earth would go into a holding pattern if I weren't there for the day.

I would never have bought anything just because it was practical, wouldn't show soil or was guaranteed to last a lifetime.

Instead of wishing away nine months of pregnancy, I'd have cherished every moment realizing that the wonderment growing inside me was the only chance in life to assist God in a miracle.

When my kids kissed me impetuously, I would never have said, "Later. Now go get washed up for dinner."

There would have been more "I love yous" ... more "I'm sorrys" .....but mostly, given another shot at life, I would seize every minute.....look at it and really see it ... live it ... and never give it back.

When need is greatest, God is nearest.

Nancy Underwood, is well known in California and throughout the industrial field, where her expertise in occupational safety and awareness of hazardous materials have earned her awards from such publications as The *World's Who's Who of Women*, *Who's Who in the West*, and *Who's Who of American Women*. A U.S. Congressional Advisory Board has also commended her in recognition of her outstanding services as a California State Advisor in the area of safety. Ms. Underwood's recognition on the global stage is also on the rise, as she continues to work in the safety and environmental field in many countries overseas.

Nancy Underwood
President
Underwood Loss Control

Contact:

Underwood Loss Control
6245 Bristol Parkway, # 105
Culver City, CA 90230

Phone: (310) 743-0220
Fax: (310) 743-0223
Email: ulc@earthlink.net

Nancy Underwood
President, Underwood Loss Control, Inc.

Sharon: *Nancy, you moved many mountains to get where you are in the male-dominated environmental and occupational safety business. Not only has the work of your firm made an important contribution to helping many organizations in this country to meet their environmental and safety goals, it has also done the same many countries overseas. Tell us about Underwood Loss Control and how you went global.*

Nancy: Underwood Loss Control (ULC), Inc. was founded in 1982. The firm began as an Occupational Health and Safety consulting firm and has progressed to a full service environmental and construction management firm specializing in site investigation and remediation, including underground storage tanks and hazardous materials. ULC provides consulting services to corporations, municipalities, to the State of California, and to various federal government agencies.

Sharon: *How did you prepare academically to get in such an unusual field?*

Nancy: It is sort of a long story but an important one to understand how I was able to break through in my field. My first degree was a Bachelor of Science from California State University in Environmental Occupational Health and Safety Engineering. Subsequently, I earned teaching credentials from "Cal State" in Public Safety, Accident Prevention, and Traffic Safety. In 1978, I received a certificate in Environmental and Occupational Toxicology and the next year Engineering and Risk Management Certificate from the Traveler's Insurance Company in Hartford,

Connecticut. All of these credentials have played an important role in enabling me to do what I do.

Sharon: *Among your various qualifications, which have been the most important in enabling you to break through in your consulting field?*

Nancy: Each of my qualifications has been a building block in helping me to take the small smart steps to lead to where I am today. However, I really broke through the glass ceiling when I obtained an Engineering Contractor's Class A license, which qualifies our firm as a full-service environmental and construction management firm. My license in Asbestos Abatement has also been an important qualification in my work.

Sharon   *Are you the only African American in the State of California who holds an Engineering Contractor's Class A license?*

Nancy: Yes, I'm the only female African American with this designation in the State of California, and one of three women in the U.S. altogether.

Sharon   *What are the most important inner resources you have drawn on to get where you are today?*

Nancy: Ambition, determination, and my willingness to work hard are my three strongest attributes. I first discovered my ambition when I was just a child. I grew up with seven siblings in a single parent household. My family was poor but my dreams were very rich. I never accepted any limitations and always visualized myself as being successful.

My friend once gave me a little book of encouragement that meant so much to me. I lived by some of the thoughts in that little book. One that was very close to my heart stated: "When you get into a tight place and everything goes against you until it seems as if you can't hold on a minute longer, never give up then, for that's the time when the tides will turn."

Sharon: *And did you have to "hold on very hard?" Was it hard for you?*

Nancy: My life has been very challenging and I have had to hold on very hard indeed. I moved to California in 1967, along with my husband and daughter. However, my husband and I soon divorced. When this happened, I had to accept a job as a mail clerk in the Post Office. I did not let this daunt my spirits, however. I always looked beyond that point and saved money to go to college. After working in the Post Office for two years, I finally saved up enough money for college. I attended Los Angeles County-USC Medical Center where I earned an X-Ray Technician's license. Eventually I upgraded my skills to that of a radiologist technologist.

One day, my former instructor contacted me to encourage me to return to school to study health and safety. I knew that it was a male-dominated field, but this only encouraged me to be more determined to make a break through. In 1974, I earned a Bachelor's degree in Occupational Safety and Health, having completed a three year program in only two years.

Sharon: *It must have been very difficult with a small child and as a single mother to complete your studies, and ahead of time?*

Nancy: It was difficult. I was 30 years old, divorced, and the mother of a two-and-a-half-year-old girl, and yet, I was going to school full-time. Further complicating my situation was the fact that I had a car accident just before enrolling in school. Although I attended school wearing a neck brace, I was *braced* to get my degree! I took my daughter to class and scheduled my classes around her. I had to be organized in all aspects of my life, which enabled me to graduate early.

I also want you to know that I had help. When I realized I couldn't work and was going to be incapacitated, I went down to the county and told them: "Listen, I just had a serious accident. The doctor says I'm not going to be able to work for two years. I'm asking if you will give me assistance and help me with my child care and my tuition for two years?"

They said, "Nancy, fill out your papers—you are the first person who ever came down here to ask for help for a specified period of time. We will give you babysitting money, we will help you with your tuition, and we will give you a [welfare] check every month."

After I graduated, I immediately went down to the county office and said, "I graduated, now you can take me off assistance." They could not believe it and asked me if I was sure. I was sure, and they were happy and claim me as a success story.

Sharon: *Yours is indeed a real welfare-to-work success story. Did you immediately want to start your own company after graduating, or did you want to work for a firm to gain experience before going out on your own?*

Nancy: I wanted to gain a broad base of experience working with other firms prior to going out on my own, so I started doing my research on possible employers before I graduated. Six months prior to graduating, I was hired as a health and safety trainee for the Travelers' Insurance Company. To move to the next level in the company, as an engineer, I had to go back to school and get another certification.

Sharon: *How long did you stay with Travelers' Insurance Company?*

Nancy: I had planned to stay with the firm for five years. But in the end, I only gave them three-and-a-half because that is how long it took me to learn everything I needed to know to move to the next level in my career.

Sharon: *What was your next move on your critical path to start your own company?*

Nancy: I next joined Textron in 1977, where my goal was to end each year with no "Loss-Time Accidents." After developing many innovative and effective employee safety programs and specific accident prevention programs, I won an award as the best health and safety engineer in the company. I stayed with the firm almost four years.

Sharon: *After you left Textron were you ready to start your own business yet?*

Nancy: No, not yet. There was one more frontier to conquer, aerospace. I always believed that if I could make it in aerospace, I could make it in any industry. So, I went to work for Northrup. I knew the health and safety manager there. Prior to my departure from Textron, the health and safety manager at Northrup expressed his interest in hiring me. I was also interested in working for Northrup because it was so "high tech" and because it was a global firm by definition. I knew that working there would be my own launching pad.

Sharon: *So, you joined Northrup. What exactly did you do there?*

Nancy: I was an Occupational Health and Safety Engineer in the Aircraft Operations Division. I was in charge of the Second Shift in this division, which experienced a 65 percent reduction in the accident rate during my tenure there. The safety program I developed and implemented had two major segments: One was a Management and Safety Training Program and the other intensified the employee safety monitor system for all departments of the second shift.

Sharon: *Okay, so you conquered the aerospace frontier over a four-year period. What was the next step in your strategy to become a business owner?*

Nancy: I was finally ready to open my own business and incorporated Underwood Loss Control in 1982. Two of our main business targets for our work were the State Department and the EPA. It took four years to penetrate these agencies, but we could not have done it without the assistance of the Office of Small and Disadvantaged Business Utilization (OSDBU) in each agency. We first broke through at the State Department. We were requested to manage the removal of Asbestos Containing Materials (ACMs) for the U.S. American Embassy in Frankfurt, Germany. We subsequently worked in Pakistan, and in El Salvador. Our work in El Salvador was particularly interesting because we undertook it at a time in 1986 when the country was at war. As you can imagine, we were working under very tight security. Eventually, we were able to broaden our client base and the types of overseas assignments we performed overseas.

Sharon: *Was your firm certified by the U.S. Small Business Administration as an 8(a) firm [a small and disadvantaged firm that receives business development assistance by the SBA]?*

Nancy: Yes, we were 8(a) certified over a nine-year period and successfully graduated from the program after our term ended. This certification helped our firm receive a number of major contracts, including a major contract from the Federal Aviation Administration. The key to being successful in this program was obtaining my general Engineering Contractor's Class A license; we really took off in the program once we had this certification.

Sharon: *Did you firm have any strategic alliances that helped your firm to grow?*

Nancy: Yes, we formed very important and lasting alliances with two of our main subcontractors. One was A.E. Schmidt Environmental and the other is Tetratech, which is a large billion dollar firm. I had mentors within both of these firms who have and continue to guide me and assist ULC in global development.

Sharon: *How have your mentors and strategic alliance partners played a role in helping you to grow your domestic business?*

Nancy: It should be understood that on multimillion-dollar federal government contracts, it is often the case that small firms do not have all of the qualifications needed to perform all work elements of the contract, nor do they necessarily know about bidding and pricing strategies. In both cases, our mentors played an important role in helping us to cross the Rubicon. We cannot overstate the importance of forming such alliances, recognizing, of course, that everybody has to bring something to the table. What we brought to the table was our certifications, previous experience, and our preferential access to the federal government market by virtue of our 8(a) status. What we were looking for in return was access to new technologies and to the ability, through our strategic alliances, to demonstrate a broader base of the qualifications required for specific contracts. Forming such alliances was critical to our success in penetrating the federal government market. Often, staff within the federal government agencies helped us identify strategic partners. For instance, one of the staff members of the Environmental Protection Agency's (EPA) small business office helped our firm link up with one of its strategic partners with whom we subsequently bid and performed federal government jobs.

I also want to underscore that in order to learn from our partners, we had to put in the time required to learn, to upgrade our skills, and to obtain the required certifications and licenses. This meant working late at night, studying new information, and learning new ways of doing business. We had a lot to learn in two important areas: proposal preparation and in pricing the job. To this day, I do not submit a major bid anywhere in the world without seeking the advice of my mentors. My mentors have shown me outlines of technical proposals and how to cost out the various elements of the work. We have also received assistance and training from the Small Business Administration in this regard.

Sharon: *I'm so glad you shared this so our audience knows that they don't have to do it all on their own. We all get a little help along the way.*

Nancy: Indeed, you have to form alliances with those who will show you how to play the game. You have to play the game like the big boys to win.

Sharon: *Who helped showed you the way the "big boys" play in the global marketplace?*

Nancy: I utilized the resources of the U.S. Small Business Administration's Export Training Program (ETAP) that is administered through the U.S. Export Assistance Center (USEAC) network throughout the United States. This is a comprehensive export-training program that provides information about export regulations, financing, and other operational concerns. This training complemented my own experience of doing business overseas for over 26 years. At the same time, and as always, I also relied on my longstanding mentors for advice on how to structure international deals.

Sharon: *I understand that there is an expectation that ETAP graduates will increase their exports overseas. Are you an ETAP success story?*

Nancy: Indeed I am, as I am about to embark on a major international endeavor that will require my team and me to live overseas for quite a while.

Sharon: *Can you tell us about this new venture?*

Nancy: I can tell you that our new venture will be in Central America and will involve developing a broad range of comprehensive environmental health and safety programs throughout the country that will be based on our American safety and environmental regulatory framework.

Sharon: *Will you model our U.S. health and safety regulatory system in the Central American country?*

Nancy: Yes, we will draw on many examples from our U.S. health and safety regulatory system. There are six districts in my client country and our contract requires that we complete one district per year, by providing a comprehensive set of plans and training programs to implement the health and safety systems we will be recommending. Our comprehensive training program will provide training to a broad range of health and safety staff in all six districts of the country and at the municipality level as well.

Sharon: *Was doing this kind of work overseas part of your dream?*

Nancy: Yes, this is part of my dream in many ways. Although I worked in many countries, I feel at home in Central America. Moreover, the assignment will enable my firm to apply its many lessons learned throughout the years. It is as if all roads have led us to this and that every assignment was performed as a stepping-stone to enable us to take on this monumental undertaking.

Sharon: *You will be performing a Herculean task. Clearly, this assignment not only requires a broad range of corporate qualifications, it also takes a lot of guts. How did you become so self-confident? Were any members of your family roles models to you in your business?*

Nancy: I built my self-confidence one success at a time. As to my family members being role models in business, I can say it has been quite to the contrary, to put it mildly. However, I can also say that one of the reasons why I am such an overachiever is because I was trying to win their love.

Sharon: *Is there ever discord between your self-confidence and willingness to rely on others?*

Nancy: No. Being self-confident does not mean that I do not rely on others. It only means that I trust my judgment about those on whom I am relying or collaborating with. It also means that I trust my ability to engage in the process of preparing to go global.

Sharon: *What about access export working capital? Are you confident in your ability to do that?*

Nancy: Yes, I am confident that I can access the external financing that we require, as I have established close working relationships with many financing institutions, such as the SBA, and the U.S. Export Import Bank (EXIM Bank).

Sharon: *Given all of the work you obviously do, how do you achieve a balance in your life?*

Nancy: All work and no play would make Nancy a dull girl—and by no means is Nancy a dull girl, I can assure you! I set aside hours for exercise, for meditation, for prayer, and for fun. Indeed, there is fun in work and fun in working on the road. My daughter is thirty-three years old now. She was with me as I prepared my whole life to go global, and now that she is grown, I am free to go.

Sharon: *In closing, what advice would you like to share about going global?*

Nancy: Any woman who wants to go global should first check with the SBA to seek their assistance <www.sba.gov>. They should also check with the EXIM Bank to ensure that EXIM will guarantee loans for that country <www.exim.gov>. The next most important thing is to utilize the *National Trade Data Bank* <www.stat-USA.gov>, which provides comprehensive economic, social, and political information on most foreign countries.

*   *   *

In Tbilisi, It's Betsy's Place: An Isle of Elegance Amid Byzantine Chaos

By Alessandra Stanley
New York Times Service

TBILISI, Georgia — In Casablanca, everybody went to Rick's. In Tbilisi, they go to Betsy's Place.

On a narrow, steep and tumbling side street of the once raffish and now mostly ravaged capital of Georgia, there is a small hotel. Diplomats, World Bank analysts and consultants stay there. Prominent locals and visiting jet-setters drop in for dinner. In June, Shahpari Khashoggi, the wife of Adnan Khashoggi, the Saudi financier and former arms trader, had dinner there with the owner, daintily sampling logo and satsivi by candlelight on the rooftop terrace.

The proprietor of the elegant Betsy's Place is in her own way as improbable an expatriate as the one played by Humphrey Bogart. Betsy is actually Elizabeth Haskell, an exquisitely dressed, immaculably coiffed former Baltimore debutante in her late 50s who on most days looks as if she had just stepped out of a garden club meeting in the Georgetown district of Washington.

"I wanted to call the hotel '21,' as in its address, 21 Gogibashvili, you know, like '21' in New York," she said in brisk, upper-class tones. "But people kept calling it 'Betsy's Place,' and I figured I had better register before somebody stole the name."

The story behind Betsy's Place could not be more different from the founding of "21" in New York. In 1994, Tbilisi, not yet recovered from civil war with neighboring Abkhazia, was in the throes of a violent power struggle between rival private armies. It was under curfew, with no heat, running water or electricity and with gunfire echoing through the night.

That summer, Kalashnikov-toting paramilitary men loyal to Jaba Ioseliani, a charismatic bandit-rebel who is now in jail, took over the lobby of the Metechi Palace, a huge luxury hotel built by an Austrian chain in 1989. Combatants had a habit of spraying the lobby with bullets, leading the U.S. Embassy to decide it would be imprudent to continue putting up its visiting officials and humanitarian aid workers there.

"The embassy asked me if I could find someplace else," Ms. Haskell, who was then running her own real-estate company here, recalled. "I had this wonderful house for rent, with bathrooms on every floor, so I said yes." Three weeks later, she opened for business.

Peace has been restored under President Eduard Shevardnadze. Prosperity, however, remains elusive. Foreign investors are not yet flocking in droves, and the occupancy rate of the $300-a-night Metechi Palace hovers at 20 percent.

The 13 rooms and two suites that make up Betsy's Place are booked months in advance and cost $100 to $130 a night. Guests are greeted by cool stone and gleaming hardwood floors, plush Oriental carpets, antique furniture and fresh flowers.

Ms. Haskell installed a diesel-fueled furnace to provide heat and hot water for showers — one of the few houses in Tbilisi with such a luxury. She has a generator — and candles — to deal with the frequent power failures. Telephone service in Tbilisi remains erratic, and guests cannot make trans-Atlantic calls from their rooms. Ms. Haskell is arranging to provide all guests with rented cellular phones.

She said she still had to ship in most supplies from Turkey, even cleaning products, sheets, towels and glassware. "The cost of business is high because everything is imported," she said. "It's like living on Nantucket."

With Georgian and foreign backers, she has also opened a swanky private business club, the Transcaucasian, in a stately mansion belonging to the composers' union. Worried that hotel guests will weary of the local fare of eggplant, tomatoes and cucumber, she is also starting her own farm to grow peas and asparagus for her restaurant. "You can get bored with the food," she said with a small sigh. "There isn't much variety." Ms. Haskell, a former labor organizer who is divorced and was widowed twice, has led a varied life, but she had never run her own

See PLACE, Page 15

Elizabeth Haskell in her elegant, small hotel in Tbilisi.
James Hill/The New York Times

Betsy Haskell
Proprietor
Betsy's Guest House

Contact:

Betsy's Guest House

Gogebashvili 21
Tblisi, Republic of Georgia

Phone: (995- 32) 98-95-53
Fax (995-32) 001237
Email: betsy@2121.ge
Web: www.betsyshotel.com

Betsy Haskell

Proprietor of Betsy's Guest House
Tbilisi, Republic of Georgia

Sharon: *When I learned that I would be traveling to Georgia [May 2000], I asked all of my friends who travel a lot in Eastern Europe whether they knew any interesting American women doing business there whom I could interview for my book. Everybody told me that I had to meet Betsy! When my taxi driver found your hotel in an interesting Byzantine looking part of town I looked around me and instantly knew that there was an interesting story behind this hotel and its owner.*

We have all seen the movie Casablanca. What intrigued us and captured our imagination about that movie was that it was in a mysterious far off place in the world and that "Rick" [in the movie] was able to maneuver through all of the chaos and local intrigues to operate his business. I think that the article written in the International Herald Tribune about you captures the essence of that sprit and gives us a glimpse into what it like to operate in such an environment. Tell us how you came to own and operate your own Casablanca.

Sharon: *How did you come to live in Georgia?*

Betsy: I came here as an economic development consultant to the government of Georgia. Once I started working in the country, I could see its possibilities for future growth and development. I could not walk away from the excitement I felt to be a part of this new economic development experiment and challenge. So I decided to stay in Georgia and to open a guesthouse. When I opened

Betsy's Guest House, I moved out of the realm of the theoretical into the real world of economic development.

Sharon: *I understand that Georgia used to be the richest and most successful country within the Soviet Union. Is that right?*

Betsy: Yes, that is right. Georgia is a country with a very long and noble history. When you walk down the streets of its capital Tbilisi, for instance, you see the many majestic and historical buildings that bespeak of its glory times. When you meet the many educated scientists and well-trained people of the country you cannot help to perceive that it is not only a country of the past but one that must have the potential for growth and development in the future. It is this perception that drew me into Georgia and that made me want to be a part of its future. While it is a perception that I would like to hold onto, it is sometimes difficult as I watch the country slide down the slippery slope of corruption and graft.

Sharon: *To put your experience into perspective, had you worked extensively overseas prior to working and living in Georgia in 1992?*

Betsy: No, I had never worked overseas prior to coming to Georgia, although I had traveled extensively in other Soviet republics.

Sharon: *Given that you had not worked overseas before you established your business in Georgia, wasn't establishing your business in Georgia, of all places, a big leap? Weren't you afraid?*

Betsy: No, it never dawned on me to be worried.

Sharon: *This is what other women really want to know about—how is it that you weren't worried, how did you have that much self-confidence?*

Betsy: There were a number of factors that contributed to my self-confidence about starting my hotel business in Georgia. First, I was able to hire two American men who were living here in Georgia who had had prior hotel management experience. They helped me set up the operations and all of the required management systems. The whole thing only took three weeks.

Sharon: *Did you have any concern about hiring these men and relying on their advice, even though they knew more about how operating a hotel than you?*

Betsy: No, I didn't have any concern. Anyway, I knew that I could always fire them if need be. In fact, I did have to fire them before long because they were alcoholics, as it turned out. Before they left, however, I learned a great deal from them—you could say that they transferred their technology to me.

Sharon: *How did you obtain financing?*

Betsy: It didn't cost much to start the business here at that time; in fact, it only cost three months' rent in advance, so, I mean, what was the downside? You lose $1500 or $4500 or something. It wasn't a big deal.

As there weren't any other Western investors here at the time, I was very much encouraged by the government to make this investment. The government believed that it would serve as a positive example to help attract other Western investments. The Georgians looked on this as a very positive thing for the country, and to a certain extent, they still do, because believe it or not, this is still one of the few profitable Western businesses in Georgia today.

Sharon: *Did you become profitable right away?*

Betsy: Yes, we have been profitable from the first day we opened.

Sharon: *Who are your clients? Are they mostly foreigners?*

Betsy: My clients are all foreigners, and almost 70 percent are from the States. And among them, 60 to 70 percent are consultants.

Sharon: *You are already famous, so I guess all the foreigners know where to stay when they are in Tblisi.*

Betsy: They know where to come, and it's a very different kind of experience. In a strange country, and believe me Georgia is strange, it is very important to provide this sort of American sense here where everybody speaks English and where the place looks and feels Western. It is a feeling that my visitors don't get anywhere else in the former Soviet Union, actually.

Sharon: *You have obviously accomplished a lot and created a positive example through your hotel. How do measure your success at this point?*

Betsy: I have always measured my success in terms of profitability and fun—I always wanted to be profitable, and I always wanted to have fun in the process.

Sharon: *And are you still profitable and are you still having fun five years later?*

Betsy: Yes, we are still profitable, but I am not having as much fun as in the beginning. It was much more of an adventure in the early days. The people who stayed with us in the beginning used to be more fun and more adventurous. Back then everybody was jumping in and taking risks and just being here. It was really fun!

Sharon: *I know the feeling. When I first started working in China back in 1979, all of the foreigners there felt very special too. We used to meet at the Beijing Hotel and strut around and we all felt that we were at the top of the global game because we were there and we were doing it. This also changed after five years.*

Betsy: The special feeling we had as adventurers was lost when Georgia became more and more integrated with the whole world. Soon, everybody started coming in. We weren't just the special few people who were let in because we were so smart. You see, that's what we thought. That's how we got to be there—we were so amazing! But then later when everybody started coming in we no longer thought of ourselves as being so special.

Sharon: *Did you always want to be a global adventurer? Did you have any role models for this among your family or friends?*

Betsy: No, I can't say that I always wanted to be a global adventurer, but then again, I grew up in Baltimore and I knew I had to get the hell out of there. I knew I had to get out and do things and see other places.

Sharon: *Do you think that you have always been special? Is that how you were able to do what you have done?*

Betsy: Well, not really, I think I've just been lucky. I've been at the right place at the right time. I don't know that it has anything to do with me particularly, except that I'm not easily frightened and I'm pretty self-confident. I was an only child, and perhaps that made me want to make a difference somewhere, somehow.

Sharon: *Did you have any other major professional successes before you opened your hotel?*

Betsy: Prior to starting my business in Georgia I had experienced professional success in several other capacities. These successes helped to further build my confidence.

Sharon: *You said that you wanted to make a difference somewhere, somehow—have you made a difference through your business in Georgia?*

Betsy: The whole point of this hotel was to have fun, to make some money, but it was also to show the Georgians that you didn't need a lot of money to be successful and to start a business. Everyone here thought that you needed a minimum of $300,000 to $500,000 to start a business. I said, "Look, you're crazy. I started with only U.S. $1500."

Sharon: *What impact has your example had in Georgia?*

Betsy: Well, now there are 54 places [bed and breakfast hotels] like this, just in this region alone. I think that I have succeeded in creating a positive example and in helping to motivate others to start their own businesses.

Sharon: *In addition to wanting to have fun, make money, and provide a positive example to Georgians, to what extent did wanting to be your own boss in business serve as a motivating factor for you to start your own business?*

Betsy: It is true that I like being in control, but I have always been the boss, even when I was an employee. I had managed various nonprofit organizations, and I had been in a senior position with the International Ladies' Garment Workers Union (ILGWU) for ten years starting in 1967. In addition, I worked for Pat Harris, who was the Secretary of Health and Human Services, the position now held by Donna Shalala. Pat Harris and my female superior at the ILGWU were two powerful women who were very smart and who both served as role models for me. In terms of my professional career, women were my role models. By the way, I was also impressed with the average working women who I met while working with the ILGWU. Some of them had no experience in the United States and could not speak English, yet they worked so hard to put their kids through school. I admired them so much.

Sharon: *In addition to your professional colleagues you had as role models, did other women have an influence on you when you were in the United States?*

Betsy: At the time I was growing up, our female role models were the ones we saw on television. I remember Rosalind Russell and other strong female characters of the 1940s and 1950s. Although we had some of these examples, in the main the example that I saw was that women had not yet realized their full potential. In many ways, I believed that this was both because they had not tried, and because there were many external barriers.

Sharon: *How about your mother? Was she in business?*

Betsy: No, she was a nurse, but the fact that she did work served as a positive example, given the timeframe in which I grew up. In addition, I went to an all-girls school, and when you do that you believe that you can do anything.

Sharon: *Have you had positive professional relationships with men as well?*

Betsy: Most of the men I worked for were really helpful. Of course, there were some little s—— that I worked for. But basically, I have no complaints. It was just the luck of the draw.

Sharon: *I think many women have to consider the impact of their business decisions on their husbands—were you married when you started your business in Georgia?*

Betsy: I was not married when I came to Georgia, but I had been married three times previously. I was divorced once and widowed twice. After the last two husbands died, and even before they died, as I had to nurse them during their illness, I had to take care of myself financially. I am used to making my own money.

Sharon: *You may be used to making your own money, but you are certainly doing it in an untraditional way.*

Betsy: I think a lot of women do this kind of thing.

Sharon: *I don't think a lot of women go to foreign countries and start their own hotels. You know Betsy, my goal was to include ten women in this book. Do you know how long it took me to find all of you who are featured in this book? It was not easy and in the end, I decided to include only nine women.*

Betsy: Well, to me, what I'm doing is not amazing. I don't know why I have gotten so much press from places like the New York Times, the Wall Street Journal, the International Herald Tribune, Newsweek, et cetera.

Sharon: *I think that you have gotten such press because what you are doing is so unusual. Tell us more about how you operate in the Georgian environment. Are you a member of any associations? What are some of your support groups?*

Betsy: I founded the American Chamber of Commerce (AmCham) in Tbilisi and also its predecessor organization, the International Chamber of Commerce. The goal of the AmCham organization is to support U.S. businesses operating in Georgia. My personal goal was to try to help make life pleasant for people doing business here. My hotel is an extension of my aim to make life pleasant.

Sharon: *Are you the only woman in AmCham?*

Betsy: Yes, unfortunately I am. Even more unfortunate, however, is the fact that Georgians do not take women seriously. Although I founded the AmCham here and could run to be its president, I have declined to do so, believing that a male AmCham president would better serve AmCham members in this environment.

Sharon: *Although you have been a trailblazer in Georgia and are quite famous both in and out of the country for your trailblazing efforts, do you think that Georgians fail to take you seriously?*

Betsy: The issue is that Georgians tend to admire big business. They don't have any use for small business; they think it's useless. I have a small hotel on purpose, because if my hotel were larger I would become a target [for shakedowns]. As it is, I can squeeze by under the radar screen.

Sharon: *Although you are under the radar screen, I understand the environment in Georgia is such that there are still many battles to fight. Is that right, and how do you manage?*

Betsy: We have fights all the time. We have people employed on a full-time basis to fight these battles and a large percentage of my time is also spent in fighting the bureaucratic battles.

Sharon: *When do you get fed up with all of the battles?*

Betsy: This business is near and dear to my heart. For the first three years I reinvested every dime I made back into the business, continually upgrading, decorating, and maintaining our quality standards. This is one of the examples we wanted to show the Georgians who have a culture of taking the money and running instead of reinvesting.

Sharon: *Don't you think that their unwillingness to reinvest in their business is a psychological holdover reaction from having been controlled for so long by the Soviet Union?*

Betsy: Whatever the reason, it is not their tradition to reinvest in their businesses. Therefore, my battles are with the tax department, the standards authorities, and others who cannot believe that our money is *really* being reinvested in the business and not carried out in a suitcase, as is their habit. It costs me $800 per month to maintain my small hotel.

Sharon: *It is really a matter of caring about quality. Do Georgians care about quality, in your view?*

Betsy: They have never had to deal with the marketplace. In addition, they had a captive market when they were part of the Soviet Union, so they did not have to compete and be concerned about the quality of their products.

Sharon: *What is the prognosis for Georgia, in your view?*

Betsy: I don't know. All I know is that my battles continue. Right now, we are fighting with the Department of Tourism, which wants to license us. We are already licensed by the Sanitation Department, the Health Department, and the Department of Standards. So I wrote a letter and said, "This is ridiculous, and just stop it. What do we need this for?" If they were going to invest in tourism and infrastructure, then that would be one thing. To create another means of lining someone's pocket is yet another!

Today, I went directly to the Minister of Economics to discuss the new licensing proposal. I said, "Okay, license us, but let half the fee go to the Finance Ministry and have a specific set of targets for how the money will be used to develop the tourism industry. I want to know what they are going to do with the money. Are they going to put facilities along the road, provide more electricity, fix up some of the major tourist attractions, or what?" The major tourist attraction here is an eight-hour drive, and there's no place to stay when you get there.

Sharon: *Does the U.S. Embassy support you?*

Betsy: Oh, they're perfectly supportive, but the Georgians don't pay attention to that. Everything here is political.

Sharon: *So what percentage of your time do you have to spend for fighting the battles?*

Betsy: The Corruption Index is very high here. The World Bank constructed this index to indicate the amount of time that a business has to spend dealing with the government bureaucracy. On this scale, Georgia ranks very high. Either I have to spend the time to deal with the bureaucracy or I have to retain others to do our bidding.

Sharon: *How much longer will you stay in Georgia?*

Betsy: Well, I'm trying to figure out my next move right now. Now that I have the hang of this business, I'd like to try it in another location. The problem is that it may cost a lot of money to start out fresh in another place. In addition, I know this place and it will be difficult, and scary, to start all over in another place. Suppose, for instance, I wanted to establish a hotel in Italy, Turkey, or Portugal. The problem is that I don't know anybody in these places, nor do I have a source of clients. Most importantly, it would cost me at least $3 million to get started— now that's scary! You know, a risk is fine, but you want to have a sense that you can pay it off. I don't want to take stupid risks. I think I would like to start a hotel like the one I have here somewhere closer to home, in a place like Cuba, perhaps.

Sharon: *And what about returning home to the United States to start a B & B?*

Betsy: I tried to start one already. I found a beautiful place and I decided to buy it and fix it up. I organized the financing to purchase and renovate it, but in the end, I was scared off, and my financial backers were also scared off, by the amount of money it cost to market a B & B in the United States. When marketing costs are factored into the hotel start-up costs equation, it takes an inordinate amount of time to amortize the investment and to realize a profit.

Sharon: *Hasn't the Internet lowered the costs of advertising and marketing? I know that if I put in a search for a hotel in Tblisi, Georgia, the name of your hotel pops up on all the search engines.*

Betsy: Well, this is a very new occurrence. It is important for the financial institutions to realize this in due course as well. You know, heretofore they have had their little calculations of what it costs to take out a page of advertisements in different print media and they base their calculations on this. The bankers are basing their estimates on advertising costs for advertising in Town and Country, the New Yorker, or Vanity Fair. The question is whether it is better to purchase an ongoing concern or to try to start up a new hotel. Both equations are expensive.

Sharon: *Have you ever thought of seeking financial assistance from the Small Business Administration (SBA)?*

Betsy: I am aware of SBA's assistance, and when I was considering purchasing the hotel property in the United States, SBA financing was involved. Right now, I am in a holding pattern until I figure out my next move.

Sharon: *I know how you feel to be betwixt and between. I did not want to leave Hong Kong either after having lived there twelve years either, but when my father died and I stuck in Papua New Guinea and could not return in time for his funeral, I decided to move back to the United States. At the time, I was afraid of not having any contacts in the states anymore, but thanks to the Internet, I have re-connected with everyone.*

Betsy: I'm also in touch with all of my friends from around the world all the time. I am not sure that I am in touch with the mentality back home, however.

Sharon: *How in touch are you with the U.S. market for importing goods from there to Georgia, and what do you import from the States?*

Betsy: I am in touch with the market of suppliers through my son, who lives in Annapolis, Maryland. He helps me to identify suppliers by doing research on the Internet. I import goods like sheets, towels, fabrics, and wallpaper. I don't import heavy furniture because of the cost. What I would really like to import from the States is mattresses, but they are too expensive to import. I also wish I could import really good foodstuff from the United States, and sometimes I manage to get dry food goods that my son sends to me via courier. I wish I could import everything from the States but there are various constraints, in addition to cost considerations, such as the incompatibility of the electricity systems. We are on 220 volts here, and many of the electrical goods I'd like to import from the States are not dual system. I am forced to import from Germany or Turkey in such cases.

Sharon: *Have you ever exported any goods from Georgia?*

Betsy: I tried. I found some women who were making beautiful silk scarves, so I bought some of them as samples and endeavored to sell them to the Textile Museum in Washington, D.C. The museum wanted to buy them, but they wanted to buy them in quantities that were larger than could be supplied by the women. Furthermore, it became clear that I would not be able to guarantee the quality or the delivery time.

Sharon: *I can relate to the problems you had. I similarly encountered problems in my endeavors to export from China. I found that the deals being offered to me, as an outsider, were all mission impossible deals—with the wrong price, the wrong quantities, the wrong specifications, et cetera.*

Betsy: In closing, what I can say is that it is often not easy to achieve our goals, but it is possible, even when it seems to be mission impossible. I believe that I achieved my aims here in Georgia, against all the odds, and I am now ready to move on to conquer new frontiers and new roads not commonly taken.

*   *   *

Geetha Devi is the owner and President of Elmo Lawn Mowers and Smart IT Solutions of Bangalore, India. She is an inventor, an entrepreneur, a shrewd businesswoman, an exporter, and a mother. She has blazed new trails in the business community and has taken her flagship company, Elmo Lawn Mowers to the number one position in the market for the entire nation of India. Ms. Devi currently seeks to create major inroads in the global software industry. In so doing, she will marshal the technical resources of the best and the brightest from her native Bangalore, India—one of the software capitals of the world. Ms. Devi is one business graduate of Mysore University in Karnataka, India who is turning her possibilities into facts.

Geetha Devi
President
Smart IT Solutions and Lawnmowers

Contact:

Smart IT Solutions
No. 5 BDA Commercial Complex
Koramangala, Bangalore, India

Phone: (91 80) 5532-2401
Fax: (91 80) 533-1553
Email: elmob@vsnl.com
Web: http://www.smartitsolution.com

Geetha Devi

President, Smart IT Solutions and Elmo Lawnmowers
Bangalore, India

Sharon: *When I met you in Washington, DC recently [June 2000] at a reception for the King of Swaziland, and learned that you were visiting the U.S. from India and that you were an exporter, I was very interested in including you in this book. I think that there are many new and interesting business success stories coming out of India these days, especially from Bangalore, India one of the new information technology skills capitals of the world. We would all like to have a little glimpse into what is going on there and into how a woman thrives in business in such a male-dominated society. Tell us about your business and how you have succeeded.*

How long have you owned your owned business in Bangalore, India?

Geetha: I have been a business owner for fifteen years.

Sharon: *Are your currently operating the original business you started?*

Geetha: No. My first business, named "Ritu Tutorials" after my daughter, was focused on organizing private lectures for university students in various engineering disciplines. There was a demand from students who needed additional lecturing in order to prepare for their course exams.

Sharon: *What were the key elements of this business that you had to manage?*

Geetha: There were four key parts to this business. First, I had to identify the students who would pay for the lectures. This was an ongoing process. Second, I had to identify the lecturers who were the best in their field and enter into contracts with them to pay them for their service. Third, I had to arrange for the lecture halls in which they would provide the lectures. And finally, I had to plan ahead.

Sharon: *What prepared you to do this business?*

Geetha: There was no direct route into this business, given my background. I had gone to university and obtained an undergraduate degree in Business Administration. Before I graduated I did an internship in marketing for four months with a firm that sold processed food. I was always eager to work because I did not want to be a financial burden to my family. Although my family did not pressure me to work, I put pressure on myself to make sure I could be independent as soon as possible.

Sharon: *Were you involved in international marketing for the firm?*

Geetha: No, only domestic marketing.

Sharon: *Did you enjoy your work experience and being an employee?*

Geetha: Well, I certainly put my whole self into the job—perhaps too much of myself. My boss felt like I was trying to take over. It became clear to me right away from this experience that I am the kind of person that indeed needs to be in charge. Therefore, I reckoned that I also needed to be my own boss.

Sharon: *How did you go about establishing your own firm?*

Geetha: Going into business for myself was a difficult choice to make, for many reasons. First, my family did not have a history and background of entrepreneurship. Therefore, I did not have any immediate family members on whom to rely for inspiration, motivation, connections, or resources. Neither did I have friends, especially female friends, who were in business. Also, I come from a large family with four elder sisters, all of whom followed a more traditional career path in the employ of others. I also have four brothers, and none of them are entrepreneurs either. The lack of a social network of family and friends in entrepreneurship also means that I had only myself to come up with the idea of what to do in business. Unlike in America where one can go to the Small Business Administration (SBA) or consult other government resources for assistance in "reading" the marketplace, in my case, I was completely on my own to map out my landscape for entrepreneurship.

Sharon: *What was your strategy for mapping your course in entrepreneurship?*

Geetha: Before I answer this question directly, it is important to understand the context in which I was operating. At the time, in the early 1980s in India, there were only two socially acceptable options of how a woman should proceed upon completing her college education. She should either get married or become employed. Starting one's own business was not a socially acceptable option. I met the demand of my social environment halfway. I opted to get married, and while I was married I spent time trying to figure out how to start my own business, as it was not consistent with my personality to be taken care of by a man. It took me some time, during which I had one daughter, Ritu, who was almost a year old when I finally started my own business.

Sharon: *What was your strategy for getting into business?*

Geetha: I was trying to figure out how to be productive—not just how to start a business. It so happens that starting and running my own business afforded me with the best option for being productive, given the social and economic context in which I was living. My lecture business, which I started when my child was almost one year old, provided me with the opportunity I was looking for to be productive. I started it by being an individual tutor myself. I realized through that experience that there was a great demand for private tutoring, so I branched out to build a network of private tutors. The business did very well in the year I ran it. However, I made the decision to withdraw from it after the one year because it did not enable me to spend enough time with my child. In order to organize the lecture business, I had to work on a very difficult and odd-hour schedule to fit in with the availability of the teachers, the lecture halls, and the students. Giving up the business was another difficult choice, as it was going very well.

Sharon: *Did you sell you business or close it—and was it a formally registered business?*

Geetha: Yes, it was a formally registered business. However, in India it is not socially acceptable to sell one's business, as the expectation is that you will stick with your business all of your life once you have started it. There is a suspicion that something is wrong with the business if you want to get out of it. There is no market for the re-sell of business.

Sharon: *This means that you had to start all over and figure out something else to do. How did you do that?*

Geetha: My next frontier was a manufacturing business, which came about in a totally serendipitous way. When I was growing up, my brothers and sisters and I used to take apart various mechanical and electrical goods around the house and put them back together, as a game. It turns out that I had a particular, yet uncultivated talent for this. One day, I noticed that there was a problem with our lawnmower, so I asked the grass cutters if I could have a look at it. One thing led to another, and the next thing I knew, I had developed a new kind of lawnmower. The grass cutters tried it out and raved about it. This excited me, so I started going around and showing it to other grass cutters in the neighborhood who similarly liked it. The idea came to me to try to put it into commercial production and to market it to corporate buyers.

Sharon: *Tell us how you developed the lawnmower business.*

Geetha: The first thing I realized is that I had to move outside of the realm of dealing with the grass cutters, as they had no purchasing power and were in the employ of others who owned the lawn-mowing equipment. Conceptually, I had to understand two critical aspects of this business. The first was to understand how the equipment served the grass cutters. The second was the marketplace—who would purchase my lawnmowers. I felt confident that I had the right grass cutting "solution" but I did not know how to understand the marketplace. Remember, in India we do not have the kind of institutional resources you have in America that could facilitate this understanding. So, I started in the wrong way in trying to understand the market by going door-to-door to private homes to ascertain whether they would be the buyers of the product. I quickly realized, however, that the big-ticket item was corporations, not private households. There is a big corporate market, it turns out, in grass cutting in India because there is a law that requires corporations to maintain green areas around their work premises. Therefore, the corporations are the biggest markets for this lawn-mowing equipment.

Sharon: *Your challenge, then, was to get into the corporations to make your pitch to the purchasers of lawn-mowing equipment. Was it difficult for you to do this as a woman?*

Geetha: It took me two years to penetrate the corporate market. I systematically identified the corporations in the area I wanted to target and developed my market pitch to them. I explained that our lawnmowers would deliver the solution they were looking for to ensure that their lawns were consistent with their corporate image. In order to get into the door, I first sent them a letter in which I appealed to their human interest and to their concerns about their corporate image. These letters were carefully crafted and incorporated information we identified in our research about the firm. Our research enabled us to make the right appeal, which got us in the door to make the sale. Being a woman, ultimately, did not impose a constraint on our ability to make the sale.

Sharon: *Are you still in the lawn mowing business, if so, how well are you doing?*

Geetha: Yes, we are still in our flagship business, Elmo Lawn Mowers. We are rated number one in our product category for both quality and aesthetics and we are the market leader in the product category for the entire nation. In fact, we have no competitors, as I hold the exclusive patent on the product.

Sharon: *What is the scale of this business today?*

Geetha: Although we are definitely still a small-scale business, we have forty dedicated full-time employees, and our sales have continually increased. We are currently selling around one hundred machines per month. We believe that we are successful because our corporate goals are not just to make a profit but to provide the best possible products and customer service.

Sharon: *Have you branched out into other services, such as fielding the lawn-mowing crews in addition to selling the lawnmowers?*

Geetha: We only get involved indirectly in lawn mowing through our community service initiatives. We lend our lawnmowers, free of charge, to cut the grass of the hospitals, temples, and other NGOs.

Sharon: *What is your marketing strategy at present?*

Geetha: We market exclusively through electronic means.

Sharon: *Take us back to explain how you first understood the manufacturing process, as you currently manufacture all of your machines.*

Geetha: My first step was to get my lawnmower concept patented. Once my patent came through [in my own name], I began to look for outside fabricators to manufacture the product. Initially, I was only involved in some basic assembly, after the fabrication was done. Eventually, as our demand increased, we got directly into manufacturing the machines ourselves. We now undertake the whole manufacturing process in-house, except for the painting, which we still contract.

Sharon: *Stepping back a little further, can you explain what the process was in your country for identifying the fabricators? You know, here in America, we would go to the Yellow Pages or other reference documents. What do you do in India?*

Geetha: Broadly speaking, if you are not looking for something, you will not find it; the reverse is also true. In India, there are sections of the city where certain industries and artisans are concentrated. For instance, we have a section where the garment workers are, where the leather workers are, and where the fabricators operate. So, I simply found the section with the fabricators and approached them directly. They were a little surprised that a woman would request their services, but my being a woman did not ultimately impose a constraint.

Sharon: *How many years have you been in the lawnmower business?*

Geetha: It has been twelve years. It took about three years to hit our stride. Since then, we have never looked back. This business now runs so well on its own that I began to feel, about seven years into it, that I was no longer needed. There was a feeling of sadness, naturally, that came over me with this realization, and ever since I have been trying to figure out my next move. In many ways, my lawnmowing business grew bigger and faster than my goals for it when I started out. When this happens, it is time to move on.

Sharon: *How did you redefine your goals and diversify?*

Geetha: Once again, I felt alone in my decisionmaking and in the process of figuring out my next move. I was concerned about having to start over from scratch in a new field, but somewhere in my heart I knew that the ball wanted to roll again. I decided to diversify into a similar direction as my lawnmower business, which is essentially a maintenance business. So I decided to go into manufacturing and selling equipment for maintaining floors—floor polishing and waxing equipment, et cetera. The second time around was a lot easier than the first because now I knew how to establish a business, how to incorporate it, how to analyze the market, and so forth. At the time, we did not have a domestically manufactured solution for equipment to maintain residential floors. All such equipment had heretofore been imported.

Sharon: *I have taken note that you have used the term "solution" many times now. I find that very interesting because it is a term that is most often associated with the software industry. Your use of the term certainly suggests where you come from in India, from where so many software solution providers hail. Anyway, getting back to you story....*

Geetha: Once I got this part of my business off and running, I realized that I was no longer needed in that business, either. It finally became clear to me that I have a different calling. It must be one that entails great and endless challenges; hence, I realized that I must go global!

Sharon: *How did you chart your course to go global?*

Geetha: As you have noted, I come from Bangalore, a place from which the world gets a large share of its IT solutions. I realized that I had to be connected with the software industry and the global reach it affords. At first, I was reluctant, because so many others were in this business and I never wanted to be common, doing what everyone else was doing. In this case, however, I could not resist, as the fit was perfect. Another motivation for getting into this business was that it became increasingly difficult to hire IT solution-providers for my own business, as they are all elsewhere gainfully employed and did not want to work for a manufacturing company. So, it was out of necessity that I, and others in my firm, had to gradually learn how to implement our own IT solutions to service our own business. My staff and I went back to school and learned how to implement our own E-commerce solutions for our business. As I began to engage myself in the software industry, I realized that an additional benefit of this business was that I could spend more time at home with my husband while working on the computer. This made it easier to adapt to a new field.

Sharon: *Describe the scope of your E-commerce solution that you created for your business. Are you able, for instance, to take credit cards online?*

Geetha: We cannot take credit cards online yet in India, at least not securely. Therefore, E-commerce solutions focus more on deal facilitation. In our case, we do our marketing online, take the orders online, present our catalogue online, and perform other functions. Final payments, however, are effected through "demand drafts" [checks].

Sharon: *What are your plans for E-commerce and integrating it into your future business?*

Geetha: E-commerce and the software industry is the business that is taking us global. We have already gotten our first international contract to develop educational software for the Government of Nigeria. This is very exciting and distinguishes us already from many of the other Indian software developers in Bangalore because they do not usually provide services directly to the end-user. Rather, they are called upon by firms overseas to provide needed technical inputs. But they do not necessarily know who the end user clients are.

Sharon: *How did you get the contract from the government of Nigeria?*

Geetha: I went to a conference of women business owners in New Delhi, where I met representatives from the educational department of the Nigerian government. I showed them what we could do for them to design and implement E-solutions in the educational system, and they chose us to design a new state-of-the-art network system for distance learning applications.

Sharon: *What is your competitive advantage in the software development industry. How did you go from making lawnmowers to developing educational software?*

Geetha: I have identified some of leading software developers in Bangalore who have experience in developing software solutions for many different problems and industries. They are prepared to work with me on any job I win. My vision is to marshal the talent we have in my area in India to create a core team of highly sophisticated software developers who are capable of developing high-end IT solutions for global clients. I also want to help them go directly into the market here. In a sense, I will be marketing for them. This will not only be helpful to me and my business and to them—it will also be helpful to my country by trying to minimize the brain drain. It is not the case that every Indian wants to come to America to live. The problems for most is that they do not have any direct inroads into the market, and I am hoping to change that for them.

Sharon: *Actually, there is a common thread between this business vision and how you first started in business. You have always been in the business of matching up problems and solutions. But let me ask you, how will you identify your clients in the global marketplace?*

Geetha: My target is the United States and Canada. The first step I have taken in respect to the U.S. market is applying for a patent for the educational software we have developed. While I am here in D.C., I am also looking for office premises in order to have a marketing office here.

Sharon: *Will you be living here in D.C.?*

Geetha: I will hire a marketing representative in D.C., and I will also travel here often. I want to connect up with the Indian community here that is involved in the IT industry. I also want to make sure that I fully understand how to operate in this market. I don't want to get that understanding secondhand. I want to come here and understand the market for myself.

Sharon: *It sounds like you have some research to undertake to identify your public and private sector clients, as well as the segments of the software market on which to focus.*

Geetha: I am planning on and expecting to evolve through the learning process here. What I know is that I have the solutions. Now I will be looking for the problems.

Sharon: *Are you expecting to form strategic alliances with Indians who are already working here?*

Geetha: I would like to, but I can't count on that. It depends on how they accept me and whether they choose to let me in. I have an open mind, but I am prepared to make it on my own and to make the necessary investments to penetrate this market.

Sharon: *Do you have any apprehension about making the investment here, knowing that it may not work out?*

Geetha: Fortunately, I realized when I was just a young girl that I was not meant to do things the usual way. I read a poem once that captured the feeling that I have always had. It had to do with taken an "untrodden path."

Sharon: *Was that poem by Robert Frost, by chance?*

Geetha: Yes, it was.

Sharon: *Well, you are not going to believe this—and no one else knows this, but that poem is the opening poem for this very book.*

Geetha: Well, I am overwhelmed. I always felt like I wanted to take the road less traveled. One thing is for sure. I have had to make my own way, and there have been few who could advise me because few understood me and even fewer were on the road with me.

Sharon: *One thing that concerns me about us lonely travelers is that while we don't want to second-guess ourselves when it is not warranted, we want to heed the good advice of others. How do you accomplish this?*

Geetha: I try to take the advice of others when they are not trying to give it to me. I also don't want to make it obvious to them that I am taking their advice for fear of placing a burden on them if things go wrong. Subtlety is the key: throw in a stone and pay attention to how it ripples.

Sharon: *You are obviously a spiritual person. Share with us how going global fits your spiritual paradigm.*

Geetha: There are layers to this. At the lowest level, my motivation to change had to do with the fact that I have already mastered the domain in which I was working and was no longer needed in my business. My sense of a greater mission was over once I proved that I could start a business and manage it successfully. A silence came over me when my mission was accomplished. I pondered what to do next—in fact I was waiting for a message about what to do next. At the next higher level, my motivation had to do with wanting to create a more positive image of women in business, while also seeing how high I could go. At yet another level, my motivation was to make a contribution to my society. Finally, I wanted to be global because I had always thought globally and applied global standards to the way we conducted our domestic lawn mowing business. At this point in my life, it is time to actually go global and to explore new global horizons in business.

Sharon: *What is the vision about the global impact you can have?*

Geetha: Going global will expand the horizons of every aspect of our various businesses and will enhance our image back tremendously. It will also give us greater access to financing as the market learns about what we can do.

Sharon: *Speaking of financing, what you are planning to do here in the States will cost a lot of money. How will you finance this operation?*

Geetha: I have a budget for financing my new venture, and I also have external financing sources lined up in America as well. I won't be in a position to drain off inordinate amounts of money from my already established business in India, as I have a responsibility to my workers to maintain that as an ongoing concern.

Sharon: *Have you worked out your legal situation to enable you to be in this country?*

Geetha: Yes, I have consulted a lawyer who is preparing the proper documentation to facilitate my entry as a business investor. Overall, I am very careful in my steps in planning my entry into this country, taking small smart steps. I am also reaching out to various associations in this country to understand the advantages of belonging to them.

Sharon: *Coming back to my question about the impact you want to have as a result of your global business, tell us more about your vision.*

Geetha: I want to create a new paradigm of how to tap the IT talent in India without having to displace people. After all, isn't that what the e-solutions business is all about?

Sharon: *As you spend more time in the United States, how will you stay in touch with the best talent in India?*

Geetha: I am not doing this alone, mind you. I have a whole team of people supporting me back home who screen and recruit the best talent in India. Also, I will still spend a great deal of time in India and will ensure that I know what is happening and who is who.

Sharon: *You spoke earlier of silence. It seems like what you will never have to worry about that again.*

Geetha: I have invited the noise in, I am ready for it, and I have no power to refuse it. My new global venture is something that I have been mentally preparing for the past three years. I have also set up internal communications systems so that I can control things from a remote location. Consequently, I feel absolutely confident that nothing in my business back home can slip by me.

Sharon: *You are embarking on a very ambitious business undertaking. How will you balance it with the other parts of your life?*

Geetha: Right now my life is focused on my daughter and myself and achieving our respective goals. I will continue to support her and I know that she will support me as well. My daughter is sixteen years old now and is used to dealing with me on a virtual basis. As I am now divorced, I only have to be concerned with creating a balance for myself and for my life with my daughter.

Sharon: *It doesn't seem that you have had very many difficulties in your life, compared to some of the other women in our book. Is this true? Have you had to deal with any major crisis in your life?*

Geetha: The greatest personal tragedy in my life was when I found out that my man had betrayed me with another woman. He blamed it on me, saying that I was always working. I was indeed so busy in my work that I did not pick up the signals about losing him, and I have to say that my work was so fulfilling that I felt content. What I did not get from my husband in terms of his contribution to my overall happiness I got from my work. My overall balance was fine. Yet, when he left me, it devastated me and shamed me greatly, especially because it was a love union as opposed to an arranged marriage. When you refuse arranged marriages and marry for love instead, you are on your own, and none of your family members have a vested interest in helping things to work out.

Sharon: *How did you pull yourself together and move on?*

Geetha: It took a long time and was very difficult. I felt like I no longer wanted to live. My daughter reminded me of him every moment, which added to my pain. Further pain was inflicted on me, however, because of the way he handled our breakup. Our business affairs had become entwined, and instead of him putting things in my name, I put certain business assets in his name, which he confiscated. He also refused to pay any share of our mutual bills and left me holding the bag entirely. It has taken me a number of years to work my way out of the morass. There was no one on whom I could call for advice, especially as ours was a love union. Nobody wanted to get involved to mediate. After this experience, my biggest advice to women is not to lend their names to any of their husband's businesses, and vice versa.

Sharon: *How long did it take you to go global in your business?*

Geetha: It took twelve years and a lot of desire. Even if I never made it in the global market, however, I still would have operated my business as if it were a global business, and I would have gone global in my mind.

Sharon: *On balance, as you reflect on the totality of your experience, is there anything you could have done smarter, and is there any specific advice you have for our readers?*

Geetha: Things happen for a reason and the way they must—you have to go through to get to it, one could say. The road we have taken has not been chosen for comfort, ours [the women who travel the road less traveled] is not meant to be an easy life. But it is meant to be a rewarding and fulfilling one.

Sharon: *Specifically, would you advise women to go global considering all of the costs, including personal costs?*

Geetha: I would advise women to do it only if their hearts want to do it. If your heart doesn't want to go in that direction, don't force it. You don't have to go global just to prove something. Also, it is important to encourage women who really want to go global to be patient, and a way to do it will be revealed. This is what happened in my life. I didn't know how I would get here. Unlike others, I don't have family and friends in America. I am the first person from my clan from three generations even to visit America.

Sharon: *How would you advise women to prepare to go global?*

Geetha: I advise them to prepare themselves both personally and professionally. On a personal level, it is important for women to open their minds and hearts to new experiences and to new cultures and to approach each new culture with a sense of wonderment and respect. We have no right to disturb the world in which we work. Many women who want to do international business want the world to change to accommodate their needs. We must prepare ourselves to fit into the world. Professionally, we must do our homework. With every thought of going global, we should simultaneously be upgrading our skills, especially our communications skills, to be consistent with doing global business. Finally, I would remind us all that with every opportunity, such as that which global business affords, comes a responsibility. As our shoulders become larger through our global business, we must lend them to others who need us. We must also identify ourselves with global concerns and do what we can to make the world a better place in which to live.

*   *   *

Margaret Gatti
President
Gatti and Associates

Contact:

Gatti and Associates
106 King's Highway East, 2nd Floor
Haddonfield, NJ 08033

Phone: (856) 428-3104
Fax (856) 429-8073
Email: mgatti@gattiassociates.com
Web: http://www.gattiassociates.com

Margaret M. Gatti, Esq., is an international business lawyer engaged exclusively in the practice of customs law, international trade law, international investment law, and international tax law. She founded her own law firm, Gatti & Associates in 1992 and established the firm's office in Haddonfield, New Jersey. Ms. Gatti holds BA, MA, MBA, and JD degrees and has over twenty years of practical international business experience. Licensed to practice law in New Jersey, New York, Pennsylvania, and in the District of Columbia, Ms. Gatti also serves as an international arbitration panelist for the American Arbitration Association. She has a working knowledge of the German, Spanish, and Russian languages and is the author of many published articles dealing with international trade and international tax. Ms. Gatti is admitted to the Court of International Trade and is a member of the Customs and International Trade Bar Association. She is also Chairperson of the Mid-Atlantic District Export Council (DEC), a Board Member of the World Trade Association of Philadelphia and a member of the Industry Sector Advisory Committee on Small and Minority Business for Trade Policy (ISAC # 14).

Margaret Gatti
President, Gatti and Associates

Sharon: *As I have served together with you, and also with Candace Chen, on the Commerce/USTR Small and Minority Business Industry Sector Advisory Committee, I know how knowledgeable you are about a broad range of legal and regulatory matters concerning international trade. I wanted to include you in this book so that you could give us advice about how to properly plan our international businesses. I also wanted to learn more about your personal story and experiences as an importer and exporter. Having recently [July 2000] presented an export workshop together with you at Dartmouth University, I know that you have invaluable advice to pass on to our readers.*

Tell us how you got into the international arena; did you go open your own law practice immediately upon receiving your law degree?

Margaret: I've have had several businesses. My legal practice is my current business, which I set up after I finished law school. However, prior to finishing law school I established and ran an import/export company starting in 1986.

Sharon: *What was the relationship between studying law and exporting?*

Margaret: Prior to engaging in exporting and importing operations, I had been in international banking for about eight or nine years. By way of background, when I went into international banking I already had a B.A. and an M.A. degree in languages. While working in the banking field, in international credit analysis, I completed an MBA as well. I traveled a lot in the course of my work and soon became intrigued with the idea of importing and exporting products.

Sharon: *Did being involved in international banking give you the confidence to engage in exporting and importing?*

Margaret: My international banking background and the extensive travel I undertook raised my comfort level with the prospect of exporting and importing. I believe that I understood the international market place and knew what it took to be successful in international business.

Sharon: *You said that you had majored in languages in undergraduate and graduate school. What languages do you know, and did knowing them also make you feel more comfortable with the idea of get involved in international business?*

Margaret: I am fluent in German, Spanish, and Russian, and, yes, knowing these languages increased my comfort level in doing global business.

Sharon: *Did you target countries where those languages were spoken when you began you import/export operations?*

Margaret: Initially, I focused on importing from the countries I had prior experience in through my international banking position. These countries in Eastern Europe included Yugoslavia, Russia, Hungary, Bulgaria, Romania, Poland, Czechoslovakia, and East Germany. I had also been responsible for Singapore, Hong Kong, and Tokyo in my previous international banking position. Through my prior work in these countries I met a lot of people and became familiar with the different products they made.

Sharon: *What kinds of product groups were you initially focusing on to import into the United States?*

Margaret: My first focus was on textile folk art fabric from Hungary. Their textiles were very rich, with many different patterns from the different regions of the country. My first products were tablecloths, placemats, napkins, and aprons.

Sharon: *What was your strategy for selling them in the United States once you bought them?*

Margaret: Initially, I started with selling them, believe it or not, by mail order.

Sharon: *Oh, that's interesting. Was that in 1986?*

Margaret: Yes, the year was 1986. I had some inroads into the mail order business from some friends of mine. They were a husband-and-wife team that worked for the Franklin Mint, which is a big mail order operation. They acquainted me with the mail order business and showed me how to reach different markets through mail order.

Sharon: *How did the mail order business work out?*

Margaret: It was fine, but the one difficulty was figuring out how to get a picture of the product on my promotional literature, as I wasn't doing catalogues. Through my friends in the mail order business, I learned how to arrange to have photos taken of single pieces I was promoting so that I could put that photo on the promotional literature for individual items.

Sharon: *What did you turn to next after importing textiles from Eastern Europe?*

Margaret: My next frontier was importing silk products from Asia. At the time, there were no quotas on the import of silk into the United States. I developed my own trade name, which was "Treaty Impex." At the time, everybody doing business in Asia used the term *Impex*. I applied for, and was granted, a trade name and a registered number that enabled me to import the goods into the United States.

Sharon: *Tell us about the process of purchasing in Asia.*

Margaret: I had to specify the fabric type, the styles, and how to affix my brand label and the care instruction label. There is much more that goes into importing textiles than other goods.

Sharon: *What products were you sourcing, exactly?*

Margaret: I was focused on silk lingerie from Hong Kong. I had to determine which styles were selling in the United States and who my buyers were.

Sharon: *As you were conducting this research prior to having Internet access, how did you go about engaging in that research?*

Margaret: I actually visited lingerie stores and took note of the products being sold—their colors, styles, and prices. I struck up conversations with storeowners and ascertained their interest in purchasing my products if I could match their current styles, quality, and beat their current prices. Based on their verbal commitments to buy from me, I felt that if I went ahead and purchased the goods from Asia, I would be able to recover my costs and make a profit.

Sharon: *Was this importing operation successful?*

Margaret: Yes, we did well, and it was very interesting too. I got into all different types of silk, plain silk, jacquard silk, printed silk, and silk in different colors. The colors varied seasonally. For instance, the darker silk colors were for the fall and the winter market, and the lighter colors that would go for the spring and summer markets. I limited my purchases to a few styles and colors so that I could purchase in volume and ensure that my choices had a market among my buyers in the States.

Sharon: *At this point, were you bringing in more products from Asia or from Eastern Europe?*

Margaret: I was importing more from Eastern Europe than from Asia at this point because when the Berlin Wall fell, it created a lot of new interest in products from these markets. This breathed new life into my folk art textile products from this market.

Sharon: *Did you have a specific objective for how much you wanted to grow in that business? In fact, what were your corporate goals with regard to the import side of your business?*

Margaret: My corporate goal was simply to make money. I was laying out cash to have my products produced and I wanted to get it back. I was using the cash that I was earning from the Eastern European sales to bring in products from Asia. So, my goal was to make sales, and also to grow more of a mail order business, as that was a business that was easy to do.

Sharon: *You know it's quite interesting. None of the other women I have interviewed for this book had any specific goals. They just wanted to be in the business and do the business, and of course, they wanted to make money, just as you said. But nobody said anything specific like I want to be able to make a profit that's "x" percentage higher than what I would have made by investing in the stock market. Is this the case with you too? Did you just want to do the business, see how it went, and make some money?*

Margaret: Yes, I would I fall into this category as well. I wasn't comparing my yield on the business versus any yield in the stock market. Rather, I was doing something I liked to do. When you are doing something you like to do and you are making money, it's an ideal situation.

Sharon: *As your import business was going along well why did you want to start exporting from the United States?*

Margaret: I had always intended to do the export business, but it took me some time to find a product that I felt comfortable with and which I believed that I could sell overseas. I was investigating this while I was importing.

Sharon: *Did you intend to specialize in the same product group, namely textiles, in your export business?*

Margaret: No, I wanted to export anything that I felt was exportable.

Sharon: *How did you narrow the field down to a few specific products so you could study the market for those products?*

Margaret:	An unexpected thing happened that determined the course of our exporting operations. We brought in an intern from Germany who was a chocolatier. I met him when I was lecturing in an international M.B.A. program at a university in Philadelphia. The intern had studied the art of chocolate making and knew all about the chocolate industry. This was something that was completely new to me. I never knew there was such a science in chocolate making. He soon got me interested in importing and exporting chocolates. The chocolatier educated the three of us in my company—myself, one full-time employee, and my partner, who was a customs broker—about the art and science of chocolate making. He explained how chocolates differed from one country to the next and how certain markets had certain preferences related to the richness and sweetness of different types of chocolates. It ended up that we started to export U.S. chocolates to Latin American and Asian countries because the quality of our chocolates appealed to the taste preferences of these markets.
Sharon:	*Now you are in a new product line and in a new market as well. Did you have to engage in a lot of research prior to entering this new domain?*
Margaret:	Yes, we did our homework to be in these markets, researching all aspects of the economy in our downstream markets.
Sharon:	*Did you draw on U.S. government resources to facilitate your market research?*
Margaret:	Yes, there was a lot of information we got from the Department of Agriculture (USDA). USDA actually had a lot of studies available about the demand and global markets for chocolates. These publications, which we purchased for a small amount of money, were highly informative about chocolate consumption in different target markets. For instance, they informed us that the Chinese, who really dote on their children, often buy them a lot of chocolate. We also learned that although the quality of chocolate wasn't real important in their purchase decision, the price was important. Based on this research, we became interested in the Chinese market. Similarly, we conducted research on the Latin American chocolate market and determined that our U.S. chocolates were appropriate for that market as well.

Sharon: *And what was your strategy for finding your buyers and/or agents or distributors of the chocolates for those target countries?*

Margaret: Our first strategy was advertising in the USDA's *Foreign Agricultural Service* magazine. We wanted to put a couple of feelers out to see what kind of interest we could generate. While we were in the experimental stage, we were also in the process of gathering data about U.S. manufacturers of chocolate. Our chocolatier was very helpful in this regard. Once we identified the U.S. suppliers, we would obtain samples of their products and do a little taste testing ourselves—guided by our in-house chocolatier. Some of our operational considerations included arranging for refrigerated shipping facilities, organizing the packaging, and preparing our products to meet the standards of the importing countries. Standards compliance in the food industry is particularly onerous and exacting, so we really had to do our homework on that one. Finally, we drew on the resources of the USDA's Foreign Agriculture Service to identify distributors in different markets.

Sharon: *What were your financing arrangements?*

Margaret: We organized transferable letters of credit (L/Cs) that enabled us to pass on our credit on to the manufacturers to pay them for producing the goods, and then we would get paid as the intermediaries selling the goods to the downstream buyer. My background in international banking enabled me to work out the most beneficial modes of financing to suit my needs. My banking background also made our suppliers feel more comfortable because they knew that I understood letters of credit and how to present documents under letters of credit. The bankers, on the other hand, also felt comfortable with me in the middle as the intermediary because they knew that I understood how to work with L/C arrangements. The transferable L/C mode of operation worked very well for us. We didn't want a lot of time in between buying and reselling. We wanted everything to occur at the same time in order to limit our financial exposure.

Once we were in the candy world, we got involved in some other "sweet" deals. At the time, vending machines were just catching on in Latin America, so we began to explore the possibilities of distributing them. We found a U.S. company that manufactured low-end candy vending machines. These were the types that were free-standing little machines that you put a coin in and use a dial to choose the candy you wanted. We shipped these machines unassembled. Fortunately, they were very easy to assemble—I know this because I could put them together myself.

Not only did we export the machines, we also exported the hard candy to put into the machines. We had the three containers in the vending machines we were exporting. One container had some type of sweet hard candy, another had sour hard candy, and one had a candy with a little bit of salt.

Sharon: *As you were selling the machines, did you need to have to a service representative overseas to help your buyers assemble the machines or to service them?*

Margaret: We did not need any service representatives, as the machines were very easy to assemble. We simply shipped the machines to the distributors, with whom our L/Cs were opened, and they took care of everything on their end. One technical issue that we dealt with on our end prior to shipping the machines was how to adjust them to take the coins of the countries to which they were being shipped.

These vending machines provided a means for many little small businesses to flourish. Small firm owners would buy the machines and put them in different locations and collect the money. We gathered some statistics on the "throughput" [coins collected] from some of the machines in different locations and used this data as a marketing tool to get others interested in purchasing the machines. By the time we got this business up and running, I finished law school and immediately set up my own law practice. At this point I wanted to gradually withdraw from the import/export business and to focus on my law practice.

Sharon: *What was your exit strategy from the import/export business?*

Margaret: I had a partner who had formerly been a customhouse broker [a person who handles import documents and transactions]. He gradually took over the business and bought me out.

Sharon: *As your import and export businesses were successful, why did you want to make a change?*

Margaret: I had spent the time going to law school, so I wanted to do something with my law degree. It was my new frontier and my new challenge. Also, I should mention that my partner and I weren't getting along at the end, so I was happy to go our separate ways. One of the sources of tension between us was the fact that I spent so much time studying law and starting my law practice that my partner felt that I was not pulling my share of the load. Another issue was the more we became entrenched in certain ventures, the more I had to monitor all of the legal and ethical concerns, which became burdensome to me.

Sharon: *Upon reflection, were there any surprising lessons that you learned from your exporting and importing experience?*

Margaret: I think that the level of complexity associated with importing and exporting certain categories of goods was somewhat surprising. For instance, importing textiles was very complicated because of the quota situation and because of our strict consumer regulations that require detailed labeling and care instructions, et cetera. On the export side, as we were dealing with perishable products, there were also a lot of standard compliance issues with which we had to become familiar. On balance, the biggest lesson we learned is that exporting and importing requires a lot of preparation and research.

Sharon: *Is there any synergy between what you did in the past, including your international banking experience, your import/export experience, and your current law practice?*

Margaret: I have an international trade law practice [providing advice on customs law, international trade and tax law, and international corporate law], in which we counsel companies about the mechanics of importing and exporting. My previous experience as an importer and exporter and as an international banker gives me insights into the issues firms face that go beyond the mere requirements of the law—I have been there and done that and can therefore more wisely counsel our clients and anticipate the issues they will face.

Sharon: *Give us some examples of the issues you counsel you clients on.*

Margaret: We counsel our clients on all issues pertaining to importing products into this country and on exporting products out of this country. On the import side, for instance, we help our clients determine the classification of the product [harmonized classification codes]. One of our big issues is identifying the trade agreements that may apply to help lower the duties on importing the products into the United States. This can get complicated in cases where part of the U.S. product is manufactured overseas. For example, one of my clients was assembling or shipping out U.S. components. These components were assembled abroad and brought back into this country for sales purposes. In this case, we wanted to ascertain which trade agreement we should operate within the framework of to lower the applicable duties. We had a number of choices but the most beneficial one, we decided, was the Generalized System of Preferences (GSP), which applied to such assembly operations conducted in Malaysia. In determining which agreement applies to which operations, it is necessary to consider precisely which parts of the manufacturing process are done overseas and which parts are done domestically. In this case, our client imported steel sheets but cut them in the United States; once cut, he then shipped them to Malaysia for assembly. What you need to find out in order to know whether   GSP applies is the value added in Malaysia and the level of processing that occurs in Malaysia.

Sharon: *Isn't this the substantial transformation standard, which is concerned with which operations in the manufacturing process cause the product to be classified as the product in the end? For instance, when this standard is applied in the garment industry the transformation occurs when the garment is sewn together; thus, wherever it is sewn together is where the substantial transformation occurred. This means that the label specifying where the garment was made will identify the country in which the garment was sewn together, right?*

Margaret: That's right—substantial transformation pertains to the *Rule of Origin*. One must figure out which processes occur where and what the percentage is of the overall value of the end product that is associated with different parts of the manufacturing process.

I spend a lot of time working on Rule of Origin issues, be they on the import side or on the export side of the deal. Among the various Rule of Origin regimes, we spend the most time dealing with NAFTA. These rules are not based on substantial transformation, however. There is another standard called Tariff SHIFT, under which the trading countries have shifted from a subjective standard—that is, the substantial transformation standard, to an objective standard. Under the objective standard, all the harmonized numbers for the inputs, or the components of the product that produced, are identified, and one determines whether those inputs have gone through sufficient Tariff SHIFT, as explained in the NAFTA Rules of Origin for particular harmonized numbers. In practice, this is very similar to determining whether the components have undergone the "substantial transformation" necessary, as spelled out in NAFTA, to enable the goods to qualify as NAFTA origin goods.

Sharon: *Let's take a simple example and explain how the NAFTA Rules of Origin would apply.*

Margaret: Let's use the example of a machine motor. Our client wants to import his company's motor, which was partially manufactured in Mexico, a NAFTA country, for the lowest possible duty. What we need to determine is what manufacturing processes occur in Mexico and what percentage of the motor's value derived from the process it underwent in Mexico. Ultimately we need to know if the motor qualifies as a NAFTA good. If it does, it will have a lower duty than would otherwise be possible. To make our determination we must look at the harmonized numbers for the each individual component that went into the product and then determine the Rule of Origin for the end product. In this case, we would look at the Rule of Origin for a motor and determine how to assess the value of the assembly process in Mexico pertaining to a motor.

Sharon: *Your explanation makes it clearer why firms need lawyers like you. Just because a company manufactures a motor and knows all about motors doesn't mean that it knows about how this motor could qualify for this lower duty privilege.*

Margaret: That's right.

Sharon:	*Let's talk about the advice you provide to exporter. Do you start with advising them on which countries to focus on?*

Margaret: No, I don't get involved in helping clients to select their markets. They have done that already by the time they come to me for advice. I only get involved after they have selected their countries and want to know whether that market has any Rules of Origin that they have to satisfy in regard to determining how the product should be marked. Before the goods can be shipped from the United States, they may have to be licensed, so we are also involved in determining whether any product-specific export controls apply to the export of the particular products in question. We start by determining which government agency, such as the U.S. Department of Commerce or the State Department, has jurisdiction over issuing export controls for the product.

Sharon: *Many products are not under export control, correct?*

Margaret: Currently, that is correct. However, we have evolved to this point. Right now, I think that only about 5 percent of products that we export are actually subject to product-specific export controls.

Sharon: *After you determine whether the product is subject to any product-specific export controls, where do you go from there when advising your clients?*

Margaret: After I determine whether the product is subject to any product-specific export control restrictions, I examine both the end use and the end user to determine whether there would be any general export controls that apply to the export of the product based on end use or end-user concerns.

Once I rule out the need for export licenses, I get involved in what I call the *export behavior and import procedures*. What I focus on in export behavior is making sure that client doesn't get involved in violation of the Foreign Corrupt Practices Act. Next, I get involved in foreign country import procedure to determine whether the imported product requires any special licenses or other treatments. Finally, we assist the firm in filling out the Shippers Export

Declaration (SED) form. If the client's freight forwarder has already filled out these forms, we double-check them to make sure that they have been properly filled out and that the correct harmonized number and value are applied.

Sharon: *At what point do you advise clients to use your services?*

Margaret: As soon as the client needs to be clear about complying with pertinent export regulations, they should contact us to help them achieve this clarity.

Sharon: *In addition to compliance concerns, what are some of the other issues with which your advisory service is concerned?*

Margaret: We undertake export audits on behalf of our clients. If the client has a long-standing export program, for instance, we would conduct an audit of their export operations to make sure that they are doing things properly. We also develop compliance programs for them; generally this is a checklist that is supported by a compliance manual. We also provide export compliance training, where we go in and train their employees on what they have to do in exporting a product to be in compliance in all the export regulations.

Sharon: *What kind of services does your firm provide to help your clients figure out the rules of the importing country?*

Margaret: We are concerned about whether there are any import license requirements in the importing country, whether there any foreign exchange license requirements, or whether there are any product standards that apply to their product in that country. We also delve into all contractual matters pertaining to, for instance, agreements with distributors, sales representatives, or with agents in a foreign country.

Sharon: *Which of these services would be over and above that which freight forwarders would provide?*

Margaret: Freight forwarders don't usually advise on the regulatory compliance side, nor do they get involved in any of the contractual issues.

Sharon: *Do you have many clients who have made mistakes and their goods were impounded and then they came to you for help?*

Margaret: That concerns the other part of my practice. I do the planning side—I call it quality control. When the proper planning has not been done, then you have to get into problem resolution. Here is a scenario of how things can go wrong. Foreign buyers put a lot of pressure on U.S. companies to lower the value that they put on the commercial invoice. They place this pressure because they want to pay a lower import duty. Companies come to our firm for advice on whether they should cave into this kind of pressure. We unequivocally advise them not to, of course, explaining to them the repercussions of being involved in such dealings. We also get involved in helping firms to resolve breach of contract issues that arise. Here's one example. A freight forwarder consolidated my client's shipment with that of another company. The freight forwarder's agent who broke down the consolidation released the goods to the foreign buyer without going through the collection process that the U.S. company had prescribed, which was the document against payment mode of financing. The product was released to the buyer even though the U.S. company had asked that the product not be released to the buyer until the buyer surrendered payment. To resolve the problem we referred to the principle agent theory and were able to get reimbursement from the forwarder under an insurance claim.

Sharon: *Have you ever resolved any letters of credit problems?*

Margaret: We provide L/C training to our clients and help them develop pro-form letters of credit; this helps to avoid problems on the back end. The L/C affords a great deal of protection but it has to be used properly. L/C problems are essentially problems of quality control—such as the firm didn't look at the letter of credit when it came in and they didn't have the letter of credit amended for the terms that they couldn't comply with. If such amendments are not made, then you're outside the letter of credit and the protection it could provide.

Sharon: *As you know, many small firms operate on open account, meaning they ship the goods and hope to be paid. Do you recommend this form of doing business?*

Margaret: If they come to me in advance I tell them not to use open account.

Sharon: *If they are already in this situation and their buyer fails to pay, what happens?*

Margaret: First, I look to see if they had a contract with the buyer, because that tells me how they would go about resolving the problem. If they don't have a contract I look at the country to see what can be done in that country to resolve the problem.

Sharon: *Have you ever seen a firm get their money back on an open account deal that went wrong?*

Margaret: No, never!

Sharon: *That's what I thought—and that's why it's not good to be on an open account, right?*

Margaret: Right. At the minimum, I would advise to switch to documents-against-payment type financing arrangements—if that goes wrong you can still wind up with the title to the goods. You may have lost whatever profits were anticipated, the fees, and the shipping cost, but at least you still have the product at the foreign port and you can resell it or bring it back. You haven't lost everything, and you've minimized your risk. I know that getting a firm letter of credit may be unrealistic in many cases, so we advise our clients to go down the list from the most secured, which is cash, all the way to least secured modes such as open account. We try to determine what's feasible for them to do in the market that they're dealing in and with their buyers.

Sharon: *A lot of the things that you're talking about have to do with proper planning. Some of the women whom I've interviewed have been so successful domestically that they are eager to meet new challenges through exporting. But at the same time they are so busy that they don't take the time to properly plan before engaging in exporting. Can you give us a checklist for export planning?*

Margaret: I developed such checklists for the importing and exporting side of international transactions.

On the import side—we start with the price of the foreign product that they want to bring in. We show our clients how to calculate what it actually costs to bring that product into this country. This is where many people fall short: they fail to properly factor in all of the costs associated with importing, such as duty costs, transportation costs, the cost of their customs broker, and even of our legal services. The second tier in the analysis is to analyze whether the fully loaded import cost enables them to meet their objective of why they're imported. Next, we determine whether there are any issues that have to be dealt with in this country to bring the product in— things like ensuring that the right harmonized number is specified for the product and determining whether there are any other requirements of the entry process. Then there is the issue of record keeping. Under U.S. regulations importers are required to keep records for report transactions for five years of date of import, so we assist clients in structuring their entry records in a way to enable them to easily retrieve the entry documentation if they're required to produce it by customs. In other words, we ensure that our clients put their records in entry order number.

On the export side, we first deal with the export control issues, as previously explained. We want make sure our clients don't put themselves in a situation where they promise to export something at a certain date but then fail to get the licenses that are required. Next, we look into export financing considerations, investigating the five or six different possibilities for financing including cash in advance, confirmed letter of credit, advised letter of credit, documents against payment, documents against acceptance, and open accounts.

On both sides of the transaction, we provide our assistance in regard to the four issues of controls, behavior, procedure, and record keeping. This is my own paradigm for breaking down the transaction, and my checklist conforms with identifying issues that have to be managed in these four areas of controls, behavior, procedure, and record keeping.

Sharon: *What are some of the mistakes that your clients have made or could make if they didn't get your advice?*

Margaret: Well, many mistakes occur because firms haven't properly planned their import and export operations. If they pay a little bit of money up front to plan their export operations properly, it would save them a lot of money in the end. It's always more expensive to resolve a problem than it is to do the quality control up front. Frequently people are trying to cut costs, so they don't want to do the quality control. They become "accidental exporters," merely reacting and not properly planning.

Sharon: *Before your clients to come you, what should they do to begin their planning process?*

Margaret: They should work with the U.S. Department of Commerce and the U.S. Small Business Administration (SBA) to avail themselves of their market research and technical assistance, and financing. Once they know they have a market for their product they should work with a customhouse broker on the import side and freight forwarder on the export side. They should also work with an international banker to help them work through the payment method. My firm gets involved after these things have already been done. When we get involved, we are looking into the legal and regulatory aspects of doing the deal.

Sharon: *What about checking out the potential buyers in the country? Where do they go to get advice for that?*

Margaret: That's where their credit reporting services are useful. There are about five or six that we recommend. We can also recommend banks and freight forwarders. See my website for such a list.

Sharon: *In a few words, what final advice would you give to women exporters?*

Margaret: In conclusion, our advice to women exporters is to take the time to properly plan their export business. In so doing, they should take care to identify key issues pertaining to export controls, export behavior, export procedures, and export record keeping. If they do not know how to do this, please call us!

* * *

Appendix

Advice on Planning Export Market Entry

Some of the planning considerations that exporters should begin thinking about early in the export planning process, in order to avoid ten common exporting mistakes, are discussed below.

Problem	Solution
1. Failure to obtain qualified export counseling and to develop a master international marketing plan before starting an export business.	**Export counseling.**
2. Insufficient commitment by top management to exporting.	**Export readiness.**
3. Failure to have a solid agent/ distributor's agreement.	**Prepare agent/ distributor contracts.**
4. Blindly chasing "E-orders" from around the world.	**Avoid accidental exporting.**
5. Failure to understand the connection between country risk and securing export financing.	**Obtain export financing.**
6. Failure to understand intellectual property rights.	**Secure intellectual property rights (IPR).**
7. Insufficient attention to marketing and advertising requirements.	**Develop marketing and advertising for overseas.**
8. Lack of attention to product preparation needs.	**Prepare products for overseas.**
9. Failure to consider legal aspects of going global.	**Prepare agreements.**
10. Failure to know the rules of trade.	**Understand export licensing.**

Problem #1: Failure to obtain qualified export counseling and to develop a master international marketing plan before starting an export business.

Solution: Export counseling.

Many resources are available for free or on a low-cost basis to help exporters research the export arena. Many of the women in this book have shown you that these resources are helpful and have made a difference in their ability to properly plan their export market entry. The information below will provide guidance on how to effectively use some of the available export counseling resources.

1. Utilize export counseling. The U.S. Department of Commerce (DOC) and the Small Business Administration (SBA) offer comprehensive counseling resources. Firms should fully investigate and utilize these resources. For in-person counseling, firms are encouraged to use the U.S. Export Assistance Center

(USEAC) network. These centers offer an assistance program for new-to-export firms called the Export Training Assistance Program (ETAP). Detailed information on the ETAP program can be accessed on the DOC and SBA websites. Information on the extensive in-person counseling network of SBA's resource partners, including the Service Corps of Retired Executives (SCORE), Small Business Development Centers (SBDCs), and Small Business Institutes (SBIs), can be accessed through SBA's website. Use of these resources, of course, does not preclude the simultaneous use of other resources in the public or private sectors.

2. Know what questions to ask. In the early stages of considering export options, firms may not know what questions to ask export counselors. One of the best ways to learn what to ask is to review the questions others have asked about exporting. Most export-oriented websites have a Frequently Asked Questions (FAQs) section. The Trade Information Center (TIC) provides a nationwide call-in service to answer questions about exporting. The TIC receives approximately 80,000 calls per month and has extensive experience in answering the questions asked by exporters. Firms are advised to review these questions and answers at the TIC website <http://infoserv2.ita.doc.gov/tic.nsf>.

Problem #2: Insufficient commitment by top management to overcome the initial difficulties and financial requirements of exporting.

Solution: Export readiness.

The issue of export readiness is important because exporting is more difficult than selling in the domestic market. Firms must be ready for the challenges they will face associated with selling in foreign markets. A recommended resource for helping firms to assess their "readiness" to export is briefly described below.

1. Michigan State University's Center for International Business Education and Research—CIBER. The university has an Export Academy that has developed a state-of-the-art system to assess export readiness. Called CORE V™, it is a Windows-based managerial tool for self-assessment of organizational readiness to export. Managers use CORE V™ to identify company strengths and weaknesses in the context of exporting. Based on user-provided information, CORE V™ generates ratings of a company along two dimensions—organization and product readiness. The program was developed for simplicity of use and is user-friendly. Hundreds of users around the world, including the U.S. and Foreign Commercial Service of Commerce, use CORE V™. Similarly, the U.S. Small Business Administration has adopted this software, as have other users including state departments of commerce, world trade clubs, SBDCs, chambers of commerce, and trading companies. Visit this site: <http://ciber.bus.msu.edu/dss/>

Problem #3: Failure to have a solid agent and/or distributor's agreement.

Solution: Agent/distributor agreements.

The export planning process provides an opportunity to put the basic tools of the export trade in place, such as an agent and distributor's agreement. Key considerations in putting this important tool together follow.

1. Understand the role of agents. The NTDB website <http://www.stat-USA.gov> provides information on agents and distributors. As explained on this website, agents receive commission on their sales rather than buying and selling for their own account. As agents do not own the products they sell, the risk of loss remains with the company the agent represents (the principal). They may or may not have the power to accept orders or to otherwise obligate the principal, and as a consequence, that they might not have the authority to set the sales price or sales terms. *It is also important to remember that civil code and common law countries treat the agency relationship very differently.*

Some countries do not allow certain types of sales through agents. Other countries may require contracts with local agents to be registered and certain information to be disclosed, for example, the amount of the commission. Some countries have limitations on the amount of commissions that may be paid to local agents and some countries require that the agreements be exclusive. There may also be restrictions on the termination of agency agreements.

2. Understand the role of distributors. The difference between agents and distributors is fully explained on the NTDB website. The key legal distinctions between an agent and distributor follow.

- A distributor takes title to the goods and accepts the risk of loss. A distributor makes profits by reselling the goods.

- Distributors cannot contractually bind the company producing the goods.

- Distributors establish the price and sales terms of the goods.

3. Contract drafting considerations for agent/distributor agreements. NTDB sources suggest that the first and most important consideration when drafting an agreement is to ensure that the agreement clearly states whether there is an agent or a distributor relationship. As discussed above, the rights and duties of the two different relationships are very significant. Given this distinction, the agreements should state very plainly and clearly what relationship is being established. The agreement should also clarify the terms and conditions for selling the products. For example:

- Determine whether the relationship is exclusive versus nonexclusive.

- State which geographic regions are to be covered.

- Outline issues of payment and payment schedules for the products (in the case of a distributor) and for payments of commissions (in the case of agents).

- Determine the currency in which payments are to be made and address currency fluctuation issues.

- Provide specific provisions regarding renewal of the agreement, including specific parameters for performance, promotional activity, and notice of desire to renew.

- Establish a specific provision for termination of the agreement and terms for such termination. (Be careful with this provision. Some foreign countries restrict or prohibit termination without just cause or compensation.)

- Outline the termination process for the end of the agreement period.

- Provide for workable and acceptable dispute settlement clauses.

- Assure that the agreement addresses whether or not intellectual property rights are being licensed or reserved.

- Do not allow, without seller's consent, the contract to be assigned to another party (sub-agents or sub-distributors) to be used to fulfill obligations in the contract or the contract to be transferred with a change of ownership or control over the agent/distributor.

- Assure that your contract complies with both U.S. and foreign laws on topics such as export and import licenses; customs duties and sales taxes; relevant antitrust/competition laws relating to marketing restrictions and pricing methods; relevant laws on bribery (Foreign Corrupt Practices Act), and employment and marketing discrimination (Anti-Boycott Law).

4. Using Commerce's Agent/Distributor Service (ADS). The Commercial Service of the Commerce Department provides this service to identify qualified agents, distributors, and representatives for U.S. firms. For each Agent/Distributor Service (see <http://www.ita.doc.gov/uscs/>) commercial officers abroad identify up to six foreign prospects that have examined the U.S. firm's product literature and expressed interest in representing the U.S. firm's products.

Problem #4: Blindly chasing orders from around the world.

Solution: Avoid accidental exporting.

In our increasingly digital economy, any firm with a website has the potential of becoming an accidental exporter. This means that you may be in your office when suddenly and unexpectedly, someone in the United Arab Emirates contacts you electronically and wants to buy a line of your products. What do you do next?

1. Make sure the order is not on the denied list. One of the most important things a firm can do is to ensure that the order is not for an item listed on the denied list. Go to the Bureau of Export Administration's website to view the entire list of denied orders (http://www.bxa.doc.gov/DPL/2_denial.htm). The table provided at this site lists orders that currently deny export privileges in whole or in part. Orders are published in full in the *Federal Register* as cited in the column entitled "Federal Register Citation." New or amended denial orders are published in the *Federal Register* as they are issued, and their issuance announced in Export Administration Bulletins. Although diligent efforts have been made to ensure the accuracy of the information in this table, the *Federal Register* is the authoritative source for denial orders.

2. Check BXA's Entity List. This provides a list of entities that are suspected of being involved in proliferation activities. To make a long story short, you do not want to get involved with any entity on this list. Here is the story:

Since February 1997, the *Federal Register* has published several Commerce Department rules, which added entities to the Entity List, a listing of foreign end users, involved in proliferation activities. The Entity List is based on the Enhanced Proliferation Control Initiative (EPCI), which has been implemented in the Export Administration Regulations. General Prohibition Five of the EAR prohibits exports to certain end-users or end-uses without a license. BXA maintains, in the form of Supplement 4 to the Part 744, an Entity List to provide notice informing the public of certain entities subject to such licensing requirements.

These end users have been determined to present an unacceptable risk of diversion to developing weapons of mass destruction or the missiles used to deliver those weapons. Publishing this list puts exporters on notice that any products sold to these end users may present concerns and will require a license from the Bureau of Export Administration. While this list will assist exporters in determining whether an entity poses proliferation concerns, it is not comprehensive. It does not relieve exporters of the responsibility to determine the nature and activities of their potential customers using BXA's Know Your Customer and Red Flags guidance.

Interagency groups involved in the export control process reviewed the activities of the published entities of concern and determined that exports to these entities would create an unacceptable risk of use in or diversion to prohibited proliferation-related activities. Publishing this entity list allows the U.S. government to identify for U.S. businesses some of the organizations and companies that may be involved in proliferation activities.

The development of a list of entities of concern arises from the EPCI initiative begun in 1990 to stem the spread of missile technology as well as nuclear, chemical, and biological weapons. Under EPCI the Commerce Department can impose licensing requirements on exports and re-exports of normally uncontrolled goods and technology where there is an unacceptable risk of use in or diversion to activities related to nuclear, chemical or biological weapons, or missile proliferation, even if the end user is not primarily weapons-related.

The Bureau of Export Administration requires an export license for otherwise uncontrolled items subject to the Export Administration regulations before allowing shipments to these end users because of risk in or diversion to prohibited proliferation activities.

3. Business considerations in checking out the firm making the inquiry. Major firms around the world typically have long-established relationships with agents who have the global contacts to source anything their buyer may want from various countries. Opportunities for new companies are limited, but they do exist. Unfortunately, often when new opportunities arise, they do so in order to find firms capable of handling "mission impossible." The mission is deemed impossible if the opportunity entails sourcing a product for a price that is unrealistically low, or for providing products off-season when they are not available, or for providing products according to nonstandard specifications. Make sure the opportunity is a reasonable one and involves something that can reasonably be handled by your firm, without spending countless hours researching the requirement or phoning or faxing all over at considerable cost to your firm. Investigate the inquiry and determine whether your firm in a reasonable amount of time can complete the request. The DOC Commercial Service has a number of services to help you in this regard. Among those that might be particularly helpful in this regard are these:

- **International Company Profile (ICP).** The ICP service of the U.S. Department of Commerce helps firms investigate the reliability of prospective trading partners. Information provided in an International Company Profile includes type of organization, year established, size, general reputation, territory covered, sales, product lines, principal owners, financial information, and trade references, with recommendation from on-site commercial officers as to suitability as a trading partner.

- **Country Directories of International Contacts (CDIC).** The U.S. Department of Commerce's CDIC provides the name and contact information for directories of importers, agents, trade associations, government agencies, et cetera, on a country-by-country basis. Available on the National Trade Data Bank, it may also be useful to identify some of these sources that can in turn provide useful information about the firm making the inquiry.

4. Competitive considerations in checking out the market for the product. By reviewing industry sector information, firms can obtain useful data to assess the probability that the inquiry they are investigating is real. Useful resources that may be helpful include the DOC Commercial Service's Industry Sector Analysis (ISA) reports, which are available from the NTDB, and the Commercial Service Officers stationed in foreign countries.

- **Industry Sector Analysis (ISA).** These are structured market research reports produced on location in leading overseas markets. These reports cover market size and outlook, characteristics, and competitive and end-user analysis for a selected industry sector in a particular country. Industry Sector Analyses are available on the National Trade Data Bank and the Economic Bulletin Board.

- **Contact Commercial Service Officers in the country.** Commercial Service Officers are also a valuable resource for information about firms overseas. Firms should access this service, which is located in the major U.S. embassies abroad, to obtain the views of the officers on whether a particular deal sounds legitimate and whether the agency has any information on the firm making the inquiry.

Problem #5: Failure to understand the connection between country risk and the probability of getting export financing.

Solution: Obtain export financing.

Many firm owners have overseas connections because of their ethnic heritage. These contacts, including friends and family, can help create trade opportunities. However, if the opportunities are in a country that is having a problem with the United States, firms might face some difficulty in obtaining financing for the deal. The best source of information about whether a country is in good standing with the United States is the U.S. Export-Import Bank's *Country Limitation Schedule*. If the ExIm Bank will not offer its services in this market, the chances are that neither will other government agencies, nor private financing institutions. Exporters must keep abreast of changes on ExIm's *Country Limitation Schedule* <*http://www.exim.gov*>.

1. Access the EXIM's Country Limitation Schedule (CLS). The CLS identifies limits, if any, on ExIm's lending to the public and private sectors in the short, medium, and long terms. One of the major reasons for limiting a country's access to ExIm's financing and insurance is default on loan repayment. A negative repayment record tends to make lending to the country a risky proposition; therefore, firms would likely find it difficult to obtain financing for deals involving these countries.

2. Access the Export Financing Options. The SBA, ExIm, and the Department of Agriculture are three of the biggest providers of export financing in the federal government. In addition, selected state governments also provide export financing. A description of their programs and the terms of their financing are given on their respective websites. *Preferred lenders* (private banks) that participate in the financing programs of ExIm and the SBA should also be contacted directly to discuss their application forms and terms of lending. A list of the strategic banking partners of the ExIm and SBA export financing and credit insurance programs can be obtained from ExIm and SBA.

3. Check out SBA's Export Financing Products. The SBA's Export Working Capital Program (EWCP) provides short-term working capital for up to one year. The EWCP provides transaction-specific financing for loans of $833,333 or less. Exporters may use this program for pre-export financing of labor and materials, financing receivables generated from these sales, and/or standby letters of credit used as performance bonds or payment guarantees to foreign buyers. The EWCP provides repayment guarantees of 90 percent to commercial lenders and offers exporters preliminary commitments (PCs) that encourage lenders to provide credit. To be eligible, the small business concern must have been in operation, though not necessarily exporting, for at least 12 months.

4. Consult the ExIM's Export Financing Products. The ExIm's Working Capital Guarantee Program allows commercial lenders to make working capital loans to U.S. exporters for various export-related activities by substantially reducing the risks associated with these loans. ExIm Bank provides repayment guarantees to lenders on secured short-term working capital loans to qualified exports. The Working Capital Guarantee may be provided for a single loan or a revolving line of credit. If the exporter defaults on the loan, ExIm bank will cover 90 percent of the loan and interest up to the date of the claim payment. The exporter may use the program to purchase raw materials and finished goods for export, to pay for materials, labor, and overhead to produce goods for export, and to cover stand-by letters of credit, and bid and performance bonds.

5. Access ExIm's Export Credit Insurance. The Export Credit Insurance program provides protection against losses associated with foreign buyers or other foreign debtor default for political or commercial reasons. With an ExIm Bank policy, exporters can also obtain export financing more easily because, with prior approval by ExIm Bank, the proceeds of the policy can be assigned to a financial institution as collateral. The cost of the insurance program is based solely on the actual value of shipments to foreign customers. The cost, or premium, depends on the amount of the credit, the term of the credit, and the type of buyer. For example, the premium for a 90-day credit for a foreign company is 0.94 percent, or $940 on a $100,000 order. This premium is commonly added to the buyer's invoice. *It is important to note that ExIm Bank has no minimum transaction size.*

Problem #6: Failure to understand intellectual property rights (IPR).

Solution: Secure intellectual property rights.

Intellectual property rights refers to the legal system that protects patents, trademarks, copyrights, trade secrets, and semiconductor mask work registrations. It is important for exporters to understand how and whether intellectual property rights are protected in different countries. In the case of patents, for instance, the United States is the only country to award patents based on a "first to invent" standard; all other countries with patent laws employ a "first to file" standard. The World Trade Organization (WTO) Agreement on Trade-Related Aspects of Intellectual Property Rights (TRIPS Agreement) establishes a framework for recognition between countries of intellectual property rights. Exporters are advised to keep abreast of the TRIPS Agreement within the WTO to know the latest developments concerning the protection of IPRs. In addition to the WTO, however, there are also other important conventions and agreements that pertain to different IPRs. A more detailed discussion of the subject can be found at *<http:www/ita.doc.gov/legal>*.

Problem #7: Insufficient attention to marketing and advertising requirements.

Solution: Market and advertise overseas.

Just as U.S. firms have to compete in the domestic market for market share, they also have to compete for a share of the foreign market they are targeting. While overall competitiveness is ultimately determined by price, quality, and delivery terms, firms can enhance their chances of capturing more market share through marketing and advertising. Marketing and advertising strategies, and their cost, should be developed and factored into the export planning process. Key considerations follow.

1. Options for U.S. firms to market overseas. One option is for U.S. businesses to participate in trade shows and trade missions sponsored or supported by the DOC and other agencies. Trade missions target specific countries or groups of countries with promising export opportunities. For a description of the trade shows and trade missions the DOC participates in, consult the *Export Programs Guide*, which you can receive by calling the TIC. For additional information on upcoming trade events, contact the TIC at 1-800-USA-TRAD.

2. Options for advertising. Exporters can advertise U.S.-made products or services in *Commercial News*

USA, a catalog-magazine published ten times a year to promote U.S. products and services in overseas markets. *Commercial News USA* is disseminated to business readers worldwide via U.S. embassies and consulates and international electronic bulletin boards, and selected portions are also reprinted in certain newsletters. Advertisement fees are based on the size of the listing. For more information, call ABP International at (212) 490-3999, visit the DOC's Export Marketing Magazine, (*http://www.cnewsusa.com*) or contact your local DOC district office.

U.S. exporters can also advertise through the International Broadcasting Bureau (IBB), part of the United States Information Agency. IBB is the umbrella organization that includes Voice of America (VOA), Worldnet TV, and Radio Free Europe/Radio Liberty. Voice of America broadcasts almost 700 hours of programming to an estimated audience of 86 million each week. The broadcasters can tie a company's ads to different language broadcasts about a particular subject, for example, science and technology, health and medicine, or target the ads to a specific region or country. For additional information, contact IBB at (202) 260-9052.

Problem #8: Lack of attention to product adaptation and preparation needs.

Solution: Product adaptation and preparation.

The selection and preparation of a firm's product for export requires not only knowledge of the product, but also knowledge of the unique characteristics of each market being targeted. Considering that the market research has already been carried out and therefore the target products and target countries have already been identified, the next step is to determine what needs to be done to prepare the product for the foreign chosen market. Key considerations follow.

1. Product adaptation to standards requirements. As tariff barriers (tariffs, duties, and quotas) are eliminated around the world in accordance with the requirements of participation in the World Trade Organization (WTO), other non-tariff barriers, such as product standards, are proliferating. Exporters must understand conformity requirements to operate on an international basis. The DOC's National Center for Standards and Certification Information (NCSCI) provides information on U.S. and foreign conformity assessment procedures and standards for nonagricultural products. The NCSCI also provides a translation service for foreign standards, for which there is a charge. NCSCI staff will respond to requests for information by identifying relevant standards and/or regulations for your product. The requester is referred to the appropriate standards-developing organization or private sector organization for additional technical information and/or copies of the document.

2. ISO 9000 and ISO 14,000. A discussion of product adaptation in an international context is not complete without a discussion of ISO 9000 and ISO 14,000. ISO 9000 is primarily concerned with "quality management"–all those features of a product (or service) that are required by the customer. "Quality management" means what the organization does to ensure that its products conform to the customer's requirements. ISO 14000 is primarily concerned with "environmental management"–essentially what steps an organization takes to minimize harmful effects on the environment caused by its activities. Both ISO 9000 and ISO 14000 are processes, and not products. The International Standards Organization (ISO) <http://www.iso.ch.> and the American National Standards Institute (ANSI). <*http://www.ansi.org*> provide detailed information about standards.

3. Product engineering and redesign. The factors that may necessitate re-engineering or redesign of U.S. products may include differences in electrical and measurement systems. While other considerations in the export planning process may overwhelm these engineering and design issues, they are important nevertheless and have a bearing on costs.

4. Branding, labeling, and packaging. Cultural considerations and customs may influence branding, labeling, and package considerations. For instance, the following questions might arise:

- Are certain colors used on labels and packages attractive or offensive?

- Do labels have to be in the local language?

- Must each item be labeled individually?

- What images should be used for advertising purposes?

- Are name brands important?

5. Installation. Another important element of product preparation is to ensure that the product can be easily installed in the foreign location. The need for specially trained technicians or engineers to help install the product may be problematic. Pre-assembly and/or pre-testing before shipping might be recommend. Payments may be held up contingent on product assembly. Exporters need to know they may also consider providing training or providing manuals that have been translated into the local language along with the product.

6. Warranties. In order to compete with competitors in the market, firms may have to include warranties on their products. Levels of expectation for warranties vary from one country to the next depending upon a country's level of development, the activism of consumer groups, local standards of production quality, and other related factors. The firm's market research should reveal this information so that the export plan can factor in the proper warranty considerations.

7. Servicing. Foreign consumers want to know whether they can access spare parts, technicians who can service the product, and distributors of the products in their countries. Exporters have a number of options for addressing these concerns. For instance, they can engage a local organization to service the product, or train local distributors. A more expensive option involves stationing service personnel in the country or entering strategic alliances with other firms operating in the country that have similar servicing needs. These and other options should be carefully considered when formulating an export plan.

Problem #9: Failure to obtain legal advice.

Solution: Get legal advice.

The export planning process provides an opportunity for firms to consider whether they know how to stay out of trouble and how to optimize their position when formulating contractual agreements before they begin exporting. It is virtually impossible for any firm, no matter how big or small, to know all of the laws that pertain to exporting from the United States, as well as the relevant laws of other countries. Still, measures can be taken by firms in the planning process to minimize the probability that they will make unnecessary errors that have grave legal consequences:

1. Utilize SBA's ELAN service. Under the Export Legal Assistance Network (ELAN), your local SBA office can arrange a free initial consultation with an attorney to discuss international trade questions. This service is made possible through an agreement among the Federal Bar Association, the SBA, and the U.S. Department of Commerce (DOC). Questions may include contract negotiation, agent/distributor agreements, export licensing requirements, credit collection procedures, documentation, and much more. A comprehensive list of regional coordinators who can refer you to a participating attorney can be found on the National Export Directory. ELAN also has an Internet home page that contains the ground rules for consultations, and the names and numbers of all of ELAN's regional contacts.

2. Consult the Commerce/ITA Legal webpage. The DOC's International Trade Administration's (ITA) legal website contains papers, memoranda, speeches, and other materials on international trade and investment law, with a focus on export and investment issues such as transborder bribery. A list of the legal documents available on the website is provided at <http://www.ita.doc.gov/legal/>.

3. Consult private lawyers, such as Gatti & Associates.

Problem #10: Failure to understand export licensing.

Solution: Ascertain whether an export license is required.

Businesses that are new to exporting often confuse state and local regulations with the legal requirements of exporting. When we talk about export licensing, we are not talking about a firm's business registration in their locality. Rather, we are referring to the body of federal law that requires an export license for certain categories of goods depending upon where the goods are going, who will receive the goods, their end-use, and other issues. Such licenses are required, in a limited number of cases, to protect our national security concerns. For more information on this subject, contact the U.S. Department of Commerce's Bureau of Export Administration at (202) 482-2000.

Sharon T. Freeman, Ph.D.

Dr. Freeman has had a long and distinguished international career. Her first international assignment was with the firm Booz, Allen & Hamilton. She later became the Private Sector Advisor in the U.S. International Development Cooperation Agency (IDCA); the Assistant Director of the Trade Development Program (now the Trade Development Agency); and later, the Regional Director for Asia of the then-TDP. After serving in a Diplomatic capacity with TDP in Hong Kong for five years starting in 1981, Dr. Freeman got in touch with her entrepreneurial sprit and opened her consulting firm, Lark-Horton Connections, in Hong Kong 1985. The rest is history; since 1985, she has performed ground breaking assignments throughout Asia, Europe, Latin America, Africa, the Middle East—in over 100 countries to date. Recently, she has focused on performing assignments in Eastern Europe, including recent export development-related assignments in Bosnia Herzegovina, Russia, the Republic of Georgia, Latvia, Poland, Kazakhstan, to name a few. In many of her assignments, which focus on formulating new and innovative development approaches for countries in transition, she often addresses the question of how to accelerate the pace of exporting among firms. Her lifelong commitment to developing strategies to help "grow" exporters, especially among small, minority, and immigrant-owned firms, motivated her to compile the stories in this book—as did the frequently raised questions of many of her clients, colleagues, and friends about how she got started in and continues to thrive in business in the international arena.

Dr. Freeman holds undergraduate degrees in Cognitive Psychology and History from Carnegie-Mellon University, as well as a Masters of Science in Public Management and Policy from Carnegie-Mellon. Her Ph.D. is in Applied Management and Decision Sciences from Walden University. She recently obtained a Certificate in Online Instruction from the Walden Institute. She serves in a number of advisory capacities including as the Vice Chair of the Industry Sector Advisory Committee on Small and Minority Business to advise the Secretary of Commerce and the U.S. Trade Representative on Trade policy matters affecting this constituency (ISAC #14). She also serves as an Industrial Functional Advisor to the Secretary of Commerce on E-Commerce; as a member of the Maryland District Export Council (DEC); and as the Vice Chair of the International Committee of the District of Columbia's Chamber of Commerce.

Dr. Freeman invites you to join her newly formed *All American Small Business Exporters Association (AASBEA)*, which is dedicated to providing assistance to small, minority, women, and immigrant-owned firms to help them expand in the global market place. Join our community of women, minority, and immigrant owned firms at:

http://www.aasbea.com